CO-APE-922

# THE PHILIPPINE BASES

355.033   Gregor
G819p        The Philippine
          bases

355.033   Gregor
G819p        The Philippine bases

**GLENDALE COLLEGE LIBRARY**
1500 N. VERDUGO RD.
GLENDALE, CA   91208

A. James Gregor is professor of political science and principal investigator for the Pacific Basin Project of the Institute of International Studies, University of California, Berkeley. He is the author of numerous books, including, for the Ethics and Public Policy Center, *Crisis in the Philippines* (1984), *The Republic of China and U.S. Policy* (1983, with Maria Hsia Chang), and the forthcoming *Arming the Dragon*, a study of U.S. military relations with the People's Republic of China (fall 1987).

Virgilio Aganon is assistant professor of geography at the University of the Philippines, Quezon City.

Elmo R. Zumwalt, Jr., retired from the Navy in 1974 after a distinguished career that culminated in the position of chief of naval operations. He now heads a firm that provides advice in such areas as foreign and defense policy, strategic planning, and overseas business operations.

# THE PHILIPPINE BASES

## U.S. Security at Risk

A. James Gregor
and
Virgilio Aganon

Foreword by
Admiral Elmo R. Zumwalt, Jr.

ETHICS AND PUBLIC POLICY CENTER

355.033
G819p

THE **ETHICS AND PUBLIC POLICY CENTER,** established in 1976, conducts a program of research, writing, publications, and conferences to encourage debate on domestic and foreign policy issues among religious, educational, academic, business, political, and other leaders. A nonpartisan effort, the Center is supported by contributions (which are tax deductible) from foundations, corporations, and individuals. The authors alone are responsible for the views expressed in Center publications. The founding president of the Center is **Ernest W. Lefever.**

**Library of Congress Cataloging-in-Publication Data**
Gregor, A. James (Anthony James), 1929–
  The Philippine bases.
  Includes index.
  1. Military bases, American—Philippines.
2. Philippines—Strategic aspects.  3. Philippines—
Military relations—United States.  4. United States—Military
relations—Philippines.  5. United States—
Foreign relations—Philippines.  6. Philippines—
Foreign relations—United States.  7. United States—
Foreign relations—1981–  .  8. Philippines—History—
1986–  .  I. Aganon, Virgilio.  II. Title.
UA26.P6G74  1987        355'.0330599        87-8910
ISBN 0-89633-110-5
ISBN 0-89633-111-3 (pbk.)

**Distributed by arrangement with:**
University Press of America, Inc.
4720 Boston Way
Lanham, MD 20706

3 Henrietta Street
London WC2E 8LU England

© 1987 by the Ethics and Public Policy Center. All rights reserved.
Printed in the United States of America.

**Ethics and Public Policy Center**
1030 Fifteenth Street N.W.
Washington, D.C. 20005
(202) 682-1200

4/88

*This book is dedicated to
the people of the Philippines.*

# Contents

# Foreword

## Admiral Elmo R. Zumwalt, Jr.

SPEAKING IN VLADIVOSTOK, a Soviet port on the Sea of Japan, in July 1986, Premier Mikhail Gorbachev challenged the United States for dominance in East Asia. A primary Soviet tactic in pursuit of this goal is to drive a wedge between the United States and its allies in the region.

Nowhere would the success of this tactic have more ominous consequences than in the Philippines. And nowhere do internal problems make an ally more vulnerable to multiple pressures. President Corazon Aquino's government labors under crushing burdens of threatened economic collapse (in 1984 inflation reached 50 per cent, industrial output fell to 50 per cent of capacity, the GNP fell by 10 per cent, and un- or under-employment was 60 per cent) and a dangerous Communist armed insurgency. These problems are exacerbated by divisions within the government and strong anti-military, anti-American, and anti-foreign-trade currents both within and outside the government. Aquino's hand was strengthened considerably when the Philippine people resoundingly approved her new constitution in February 1987. But the survival of her government and of a pro-American outlook is by no means assured.

Were the anti-American elements to prevail, the U.S.-Philippine Military Bases Agreement would not be renewed when it expires in 1991, and the United States would lose its use of naval and air facilities on the islands. With this loss, the security situation would change dramatically: Soviet initiatives in the South Pacific would have much more dangerous implications. As things stand now, however well entrenched the Soviet Union might become in the region, the presence of U.S. forces will continue to jeopardize its supply lines and freedom of movement. But without the Philippine facilities, U.S. forces would no longer be as readily available, and the U.S. deterrent to Soviet military moves would be seriously impaired.

The U.S. military presence is important not only to deter Soviet activities in the region but also as a constraint upon local conflict. The South China Sea is the site of a jumble of jurisdictional claims and counterclaims. Beijing, Hanoi, Taipei, Manila, and other regional actors have asserted their rights to various land fragments and sea and seabed resources, including oil, and many of these claims overlap.

If the Aquino government fails to stimulate the economy and to put down the insurgency, it will be under increased pressure to move toward the left and adopt an anti-American posture. By so doing it would doubtless pick up support among many intellectuals, journalists, labor groups, "progressive" church groups, and others who take a more radical stance.

A. James Gregor and Virgilio Aganon assert that "the United States must do whatever it can" to prevent these developments. We must help this critically important ally with its economic, political, and military problems without compromising its sovereignty.

In this concise, highly informative study, Gregor and Aganon show why the naval and air facilities at Subic Bay and Clark Field in the Philippines are crucial to U.S. Pacific strategy and to stability in the region. They survey all proposed alternatives, including the expansion of other U.S. bases in the region and the building of new ones. And they convincingly conclude that the comprehensiveness and geographical advantages of the Philippine bases could be duplicated elsewhere only at huge expense and difficulty, if at all.

I hope this book will be widely pondered in Congress, in policy-making circles, and by many other Americans who recognize the vital importance of stability in the Western Pacific. Naval strategists agree that the loss of U.S. bases in South Vietnam, particularly Cam Ranh Bay, was a grave setback; their use by Soviet naval and air forces was a far more serious development; the loss of U.S. bases in the Philippines while Soviet forces remain in Vietnam would be a catastrophe.

# *Chronology*

| | |
|---|---|
| 1898 | U.S. defeats Spain in Manila Bay; Philippine Islands transferred to U.S. |
| 1899 | Revolutionary forces declare Philippine independence; long period of warfare begins that leaves legacy of hatred for U.S. |
| 1934 | Tydings-McDuffie Act promises independence to Philippines in 1945, after ten years of self-government under U.S. tutelage |
| 1935 | Philippine commonwealth and constitution established |
| 1941 | Japan invades and occupies Philippines |
| 1944 | U.S. defeats Japan at Leyte Gulf in Philippines |
| 1946 | Philippines become independent republic with Manuel Roxas as first president |
| 1947 | U.S.-Philippines sign military assistance pact; U.S. gets 99-year lease on military bases (later shortened) |
| 1948 | Elpidio Quirino becomes president after sudden death of Roxas |
| 1953 | Ramón Magsaysay becomes president |
| 1957 | Carlos García becomes president after Magsaysay's death in plane crash |
| 1961 | Diosdad Macapagal becomes president |
| 1965 | Ferdinand Marcos becomes president |
| 1969 | Marcos becomes first president reelected to second term |
| 1970 | Civil disorder spreads: demonstrators storm Marcos residence, riot against U.S. embassy; during visit of Pope Paul VI attempt is made on his life |
| 1972 | Marcos declares martial law |

1973   New constitution increases powers of president

1981   Martial law lifted; Marcos elected to six-year renewable term in election largely boycotted by opposition forces

1983   Opposition leader and former senator Benigno Aquino assassinated at Manila Airport upon return from self-imposed exile

1984   Elections for national legislature greatly increase strength of anti-Marcos forces

1986   Corazon Aquino replaces Ferdinand Marcos as president after national elections; Marcos leaves the country

1987   New constitution approved by the Philippine people

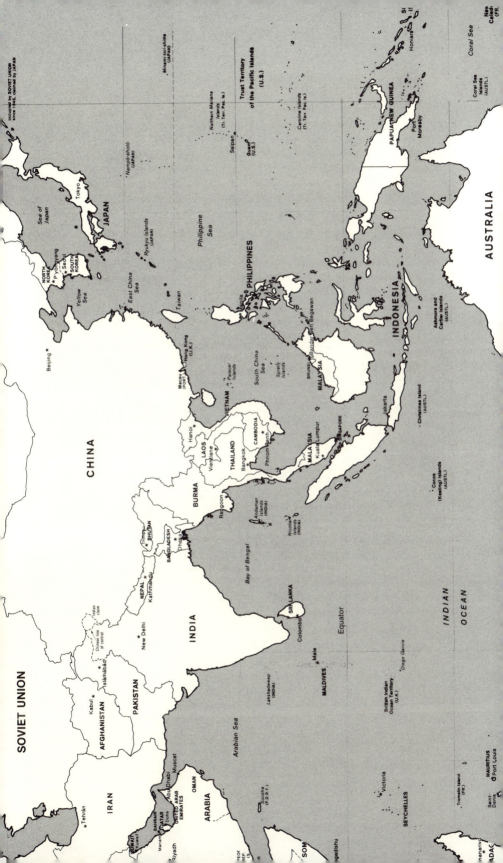

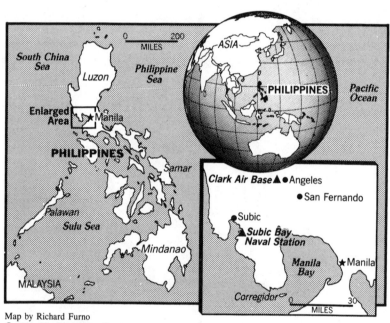

Map by Richard Furno
© 1984, *The Washington Post*

# 1

# *The Geopolitical Stage*

THE SECURITY RELATIONSHIP between the United States and the Philippine Islands dates back to the turn of the present century, when some politicians in Washington came together in a temporary coalition to support the nation's first attempt at military imperialism.[1] The account begins in 1898, with the U.S. victory in the Spanish-American War. With the defeat of the Spanish fleet by Commodore George Dewey and the collapse of Spanish resistance in the islands, the United States faced the problem of what to do with an archipelago that had been a colony of Spain for over three centuries.

Certain powers had given clear signals that with the Spanish departure they were prepared to "stabilize" the islands. Even before its defeat of the Spanish in Manila Bay, the U.S. fleet had encountered vessels of the Imperial German Navy loitering outside Philippine territorial waters. The Japanese showed a similar interest; having just established control over the island of Formosa (Taiwan) at the conclusion of the Sino-Japanese War of 1895, Tokyo clearly aspired to hegemony over the Philippines. There was also the possibility that Spain would attempt to reconquer the archipelago when the Americans left. To foreclose such alternatives, President William McKinley, after considerable soul-searching and delay, opted for occupation and at least long tutelary control over the islands.

At its very start, the relationship was afflicted with ambiguities. The decision to occupy and control the Philippines had only fitful support, both from those who sought markets for American exports and from those who thought the nation was obligated and prepared to assume global responsibilities.

1

## Admiral Mahan: A Rationale for Expansion

Alfred Thayer Mahan was perhaps the most interesting and responsible among those who thought the country had a global role.[2] As president of the U.S. Naval War College and a major naval historian, Mahan supplied the rationale for American expansion into the Caribbean and the West Pacific. He insisted that great nations were charged with responsibilities—among which the development, maintenance, and diffusion of civilization were preeminent. For the United States that meant an obligation to introduce industrialization and representative government into those corners of the world that lacked them.

Mahan urged that the United States involve itself in the world's commerce, for commerce would disseminate the critical elements of civilization that made up the core of the "American dispensation." Taking civilization to the less developed reaches of the globe by means of increased trade and commerce implied the expansion of U.S. shipping. That in turn implied the expansion of the U.S. Navy and the search for suitable basing facilities along the major trade routes of the world.[3]

For Mahan and his supporters, victory in the Spanish-American War gave the United States the chance to obtain strategically important bases in both the Caribbean and the West Pacific. A canal through the isthmus of Panama was anticipated, and Mahan realized that the Caribbean would become a critical transit area for trade and a terminus for international sea traffic. In the Pacific, the Philippines would provide coaling stations and support facilities for the principal trade routes to China.[4]

At the turn of the century, Americans were fascinated by the prospect of trade with Imperial China. China was seen as the world's largest single market, and one that offered not only the prospect of profitable trade but also the opportunity to introduce modern industry and modern political forms into a retarded economic and political system.[5] To accomplish that, the United States would have to become a major sea power, capable of protecting its merchant marine against aggression and interdiction. Thus the United States established itself in the Philippine Islands and began to construct major naval facilities in Manila

Bay and its environs, and Theodore Roosevelt and Henry Cabot Lodge began to conceive of a "new outward-oriented foreign policy" for what was to be, in their judgment, the "American century."

Beyond that, however, was a clear intimation of a specifically military, and essentially defensive, function for facilities in the Philippines. In the early 1890s the United States had shown considerable interest in the Hawaiian Islands, and Mahan had begun to allude to the increasing tension between "the East and the West" as a consequence of the western expansion of Americans. Moreover, as early as 1897, Theodore Roosevelt had written Mahan about the increasing "danger from Japan" that threatened Western interests in the Pacific.[6] It was clear to Mahan that bases in the West Pacific were needed to serve as part of the forward defense perimeter of the United States.[7] He therefore saw the Philippines as a major security asset.[8]

### Homer Lea: Defense Against Japan

By the end of the first decade of the new century, the Philippine bases had acquired a prominent place in the strategic thinking of Americans. In 1909, Homer Lea argued in *The Valor of Ignorance* that these bases were essential for protecting continental America against the clear aggressive intent of Japan.[9] In Lea's judgment, the marriage of rapid industrial development with the traditional martial values of the Japanese had created an aggressive and expansive power in the Pacific that directly threatened the United States.

Lea was certain that Japan, to establish and maintain its security and predominance in the Pacific, would feel compelled to extend itself northeast to the Aleutians, east to Hawaii, and southwest to the Philippines. This would assure Japanese access to the raw materials necessary for its growing industry and would also project the Japanese defense perimeter outward to cover all the critical waterways of the region. Any enemy would therefore have to penetrate several arcs of defensive positions before reaching the Japanese heartland.

Lea argued that technological change had made the forward

basing of defensive assets (i.e., establishing defensive bastions between the national territory and a potential enemy) an absolute necessity. Given the increasing mobility of firepower, along with the sealift of ground troops made possible by the invention of ironclad warships, rifled long-distance cannon, and steam propulsion, forward defense had become critical to the security of any nation.

In Lea's view, the United States would be the principal target of Japan's aggression. He anticipated the launching by Tokyo of an undeclared war against the United States in the Pacific in which the armed forces of Japan would move quickly to invade Guam, Midway, the Aleutians, and, most significantly, the Philippines.

Japanese conquest of the Philippines not only would double the territorial extent of Japan and provide it with abundant resources but also would give the Imperial Navy easy reach over "all shiproutes from Europe to the Far East," said Lea.[10] The Philippines are near the major chokepoints along the sea lanes of communication that connect Europe and the Middle East with East Asia. Any nation that sought to maintain a defensive presence in the West Pacific, or to assure free passage for ship traffic in the region, would therefore do well to maintain military capabilities in the Philippine archipelago.

### Douglas MacArthur: A Futile Plea for Defense

In the late 1920s, Douglas MacArthur, serving as department commander of U.S. and Philippine troops in the Philippines, was concerned about the growing threat to the islands as a consequence of Japanese expansion. He too realized that any major military activity in the West Pacific would have to involve the Philippines, and that these islands were "the key that unlocks the door to the Pacific."[11]

In 1934, as Army chief of staff, MacArthur broached the subject with President Franklin D. Roosevelt. MacArthur told the president that the Philippines were in jeopardy because of their strategic importance, and that their defense would require significant increases in manpower, munitions, and training facilities, as well as improved logistical capabilities throughout the 7,000-island archipelago.

For a variety of reasons, including a reluctance to allocate and spend the money required, those enhancements were not made, and in 1942 the United States faced the invading Japanese in the Philippines with a small and ill-equipped force that was overrun, despite heroic resistance, after only a few weeks of combat.

## The Lessons Learned

The Japanese occupation of their islands constituted a painful learning experience for Filipinos. At the turn of the century the United States had assumed control of the archipelago and had acknowledged the strategic importance of military bases on Philippine soil; yet it had done precious little to make the islands defensible.

More than that, when war did come, Washington made a strategic decision to provide for the active defense of Europe at the expense of the peoples and nations of the Pacific. As a result, the relatively meager military forces of Imperial Japan were allowed to occupy vast territories extending from Southwest Asia through the Marshall Islands, the Gilberts, New Guinea, Wake, Guam, and the Indonesian archipelago, as well as the Philippines. However strategically correct that decision had been, it reinforced Philippine misgivings about the security connection with the United States.

To make matters worse, not only had the United States failed to provide for adequate defense, thus allowing a barbarous Japanese occupation for over three long years, but the reconquest by U.S. forces devastated the islands. Manila, in the course of its liberation, was reduced to rubble. Perhaps as many as a quarter of a million Filipinos, almost all civilians, died in the retaking of the capital. Public utilities, piers and docks, plants and warehouses, offices, churches, schools, museums, theaters—all were swept up in the general destruction. General Dwight Eisenhower, visiting Manila in May 1946, reported that "with the exception of Warsaw, this is the worst destruction I have ever seen."[12]

Among the substantial minority of Filipinos who developed serious reservations about the security relationship with the United States, perhaps the most articulate and persuasive was Senator Claro M. Recto, now identified as the father of modern Philippine nationalism.[13] Recto reminded Filipinos that U.S. officials not only had failed to provide for defense but also had failed to compensate the Philippines for losses suffered as a result of that negligence.[14] It was argued that many Filipinos who had fought against the Japanese, either at the time of the invasion or during the occupation, did not receive even minimum compensation. Although the United States had promised compensation for the "full repair of the ravages of the war," it provided compensation for only 52.5 per cent of the prewar values of the destroyed properties, and that not until two years after the end of hostilities.[15] The inevitable consequence was disillusionment, and some measure of alienation, among many Filipinos.

## The Bases: A Condition for Independence

The Tydings-McDuffie Act of 1934 had provided for Philippine independence in 1944, but the war intervened. Even before the end of the war, in a Joint Resolution (No. 23, June 29, 1944), the Congress urged that "the President of the United States [be] authorized . . . to withhold and acquire and to retain such bases and the right incident thereto as he may deem necessary for the mutual protection of the Philippine islands and the United States." Because Americans remained convinced of the strategic importance of the archipelago, unrestricted access to the islands' bases became a condition for independence.

The Republic of the Philippines came into being on July 4, 1946, and the U.S.-Philippine Military Bases Agreement entered into force the following March. That agreement gave the United States the right to maintain military facilities in the islands for ninety-nine years, and also the right, through negotiation, to "expand such bases, to exchange such bases for other bases, or relinquish rights to bases, as any of such exigencies may be required by military necessity."[16] Moreover, the use of the bases was unencumbered by restrictions. The United States was granted "all the rights, power, and authority within the limits of territorial waters and air space adjacent to, or in the vicinity of, the bases" necessary for their operation, subject only to "reasonable" use.[17] That reasonable use involved the employment of U.S. forces to maintain the security of critical lines of communication throughout the entire West Pacific, and the rapid deployment and forward projection of those forces to contain any Communist expansion in the unstable Southeast Asian region.[18]

The broad powers accorded the United States, and their long duration, produced understandable misgivings among many Filipinos. Before the Second World War, the Philippine Congress in a Concurrent Legislative Resolution (October 17, 1933) had held that the presence of U.S. bases was "inconsistent with true independence."[19] After the war, a minority of Filipinos, still smarting from their recent experiences, objected to the Military Bases Agreement, not only as a violation of the new nation's sovereignty but also as a trigger for inevitable Philippine involvement in any conflict that might erupt between Washington and any other regional or global power. The critics were not at all certain that involvement in such conflicts would serve Philippine interests, or that the United States could and would effectively defend the islands at such a time.[20]

By the late 1950s, a fairly coherent set of objections to the U.S. military bases had become common currency among a minority of politically active Filipinos.[21] To mollify the critics, in 1966 the two governments amended the bases agreement so that its termination date became 1991 instead of 2046, with provision for renewal upon mutual agreement.

### Increasing Importance of the Bases

Meanwhile, the bases were becoming more and more important to the United States. They served as logistics adjuncts during the Korean conflict in the early 1950s. In the 1960s, the insurrectionary activities of Communist movements throughout

Southeast Asia strongly suggested that the United States would soon be more actively drawn into local conflicts and would require bases in the region. Later in the decade, the bases in the Philippines did indeed serve as major staging areas for troops and supplies being sent to Vietnamese battlefields.

Other more ominous developments were making the bases increasingly critical to U.S. strategic policy in East Asia. Beginning in the early 1960s, the Soviet Union embarked upon one of the most formidable military buildups in history.[22] The buildup not only enhanced its strategic and conventional forces in Europe but also gave it the capability to project its forces into regions previously inaccessible to it.

At about the time of the Cuban Missile Crisis, Moscow decided to close the gap between its armed forces and those of the United States.[23] Between 1968 and 1972, it spent an estimated $60 billion on its military, or approximately 20 per cent more than that spent by the United States. From 1972 through 1978, Moscow spent more than $117 billion, or about 28 per cent more than Washington. As a result, between 1960 and 1980 few trends related to the U.S.-Soviet military balance favored the United States.[24] Between 1964 and 1976, for example, the number of operational intercontinental ballistic missiles (ICBMs) deployed by the United States increased from 654 to 1,054, while those deployed by the Soviets went from 200 to 1,118. From 1972 on, the USSR had the lead in operational ICBMs. In 1964, the U.S. Navy deployed 300 major surface vessels, while the Soviet Navy had only 200; in 1976, the U.S. total was 175 major surface combatants, the Soviet 225. In 1964, the U.S. Air Force deployed some 5,700 tactical combat aircraft and the Soviet Air Force 3,500; in 1976, the U.S. figure was about 5,000, the Soviet more than 6,000.[25]

### The Modern Soviet Navy

The Soviet Navy over the years has tended to build vessels with heavier displacement, longer blue-water (open sea) endurance, and more powerful and varied weapon systems than their predecessors. The newer vessels are thus technologically more sophisticated and capable of longer out-of-area operations. Most recently, for example, the Soviet Navy has developed the Sovremennyy class of large destroyers (7,500 tons displacement) equipped with 130 mm guns, surface-to-surface anti-ship cruise missiles, and sophisticated anti-aircraft surface-to-air missile systems (SAMs). So large and sophisticated are vessels of this class that some analysts classify them as cruisers rather than destroyers.[26]

It appears that the Soviet Navy is shifting all its class sizes upward. Soviet cruisers have significantly increased in tonnage. A new Slava class of gas-turbine-powered guided-missile cruisers of about 12,000 tons displacement was commissioned in 1982. (In comparison, the new U.S. Ticonderoga class of guided-missile cruisers displaces about 9,100 tons.) The Soviet cruisers are armed with at least sixteen 500-km-range anti-ship cruise missiles, sixty-four SAMs, and forty short-range surface-to-surface point-defense missiles, as well as 130 mm twin-barrel dual-purpose guns.

The Soviet nuclear-powered battlecruiser Kirov class, displacing about 28,000 tons, further exemplifies the trend. The largest warship (other than an aircraft carrier) built by any nation since the end of World War Two, the Kirov has a battery of twenty 550-km-range anti-ship cruise missiles, as well as anti-submarine missiles and about a hundred SAMs, supplemented by medium-caliber and rapid-fire Gatling guns for point defense, an array of torpedo launchers, and anti-submarine rockets. Cruisers of the Kirov class are formidable.

The Soviet air arm has been similarly upgraded and expanded. The USSR has more naval combat aircraft in inventory than the United States, and their capabilities have been significantly enhanced since the late 1960s. As early as 1976, Admiral James L. Holloway III warned that the Soviets had developed long-range, land-based aircraft, armed with stand-off, anti-ship missiles with an operational range of 500–800 kilometers. The Backfire B (Tupelov Tu-22) is one such aircraft.[27] The Backfire constitutes a major threat to the surface vessels of the United States Navy and has the potential for sea-lane interdiction.

*Global Presence of the Soviet Navy*

Between the mid-1960s and the mid-1980s, the Soviet Navy was transformed from essentially a coastal defense force into a highly visible symbol of the USSR's increasingly global capabilities. Soviet vessels began to make port calls in such places as Algeria, Egypt, and Ethiopia, and they appeared for the first time in the South China Sea. By the end of the 1960s, Soviet vessels were being seen in the Indian Ocean. By the early 1970s they were making heavy use of the mid-sea anchorages near the Seychelles and Diego Garcia in South Asia and the Macclesfield Bank in the South China Sea. In effect, for the second time in modern experience, the armed forces of the United States found themselves facing a major military adversary in Southeast Asia. As the Japanese had done prior to the Second World War, the Soviet Union was developing forward-projection capabilities and military power that could seriously jeopardize the economic, political, and security interests of the United States and its allies in the West Pacific and Southeast Asia.

Originally configured to protect the continental USSR against the threat from Western sea-based strategic forces, the Soviet Navy is now capable of assuming strategic attack responsibilities. Moreover, the Soviet high command now expects its navy in time of conflict to attain sea control in vital areas and to restrict access in regions essential to Western military operations. Those responsibilities involve missions very far from its home waters.

Since the mid-1970s Moscow has used its naval capabilities to influence events in a variety of far-flung places. Soviet maritime forces were used to deliver Cuban troops to Angola. Soviet combatants protected Cuban air and sea lanes of communication to Angola, and anti-carrier forces were held in reserve in case the United States should attempt to intervene. Vessels from the Northern, Baltic, and Black Sea fleets joined a task force from the Mediterranean to provide the sealift and response capabilities that made the conquest of Angola possible.[28]

In the early and mid-1970s the West observed the Soviet fleet engaging in very sophisticated naval exercises, directing mock multi-missile submarine, surface, and air attacks that used real-time data provided by satellite intelligence. Long-range reconnaissance and surveillance aircraft supplied data for mid-course corrections, and other craft provided important electronic countermeasures against "enemy" targeting systems. All this began to come together at the end of the 1970s when the Soviets acquired basing rights in the Socialist Republic of Vietnam.

By that time, Soviet vessels had made their appearance in almost every region of the globe. To support these activities, the Soviet Navy deployed twenty-seven oilers capable of open-ocean operations—only two fewer than the U.S. Navy. Seven were specialized under-way replenishment ships that could deliver dry stores as well as fuel to moving vessels. Soviet merchant marine tankers supplemented those capabilities, providing about 60 per cent of the navy's out-of-area fuel requirements. Shore support for Soviet naval deployments came from countries with which the USSR had political ties (at various times including Egypt, Syria, Somalia, Guinea, Cuba, Algeria, South Yemen, Iraq, and Ethiopia). Auxiliary vessels were maintained through strictly commercial arrangements in such places as Singapore, Spain, Gibraltar, and Italy. From the late 1960s through the mid-1970s, the out-of-area ship days logged by Soviet naval vessels quadrupled, reaching about the same level as that of the U.S. Navy.[29]

## The Search for Bases

The major problem for the Soviet Navy has been its lack of onshore bases. In the event of armed conflict, Soviet surface vessels would require much greater support from an auxiliary fleet than appears possible with its present seaborne resources. Shore support had become a necessity by the end of the 1970s, when the Soviet Union gained access to onshore facilities in the Socialist Republic of Vietnam.

When the People's Republic of China decided to "punish" the Vietnamese by invading their territory in February and March 1979, the Soviet Union, which had signed a peace and friendship treaty with the Socialist Republic of Vietnam in November 1978, was compelled to send assistance. A Soviet task force appeared in the South China Sea, and Soviet vessels provided sealift for supplies necessary for the Vietnamese to resist the Chinese invasion. As compensation, Hanoi allowed the Soviet Union to use the naval facilities at Cam Ranh Bay, built by Americans during the Vietnam conflict, as a service port. Cam Ranh Bay provided a major link in the chain of support facilities and replenishment anchorages that the Soviet Navy has developed around Africa, which now includes the Seychelles, Socotra Island, the Maldive Islands, the Chagos Archipelago, and Nicobar Island in the Indian Ocean.

The base at Cam Ranh Bay is the largest onshore facility available to the Soviet Union outside its borders. By the early 1980s, about thirty Soviet naval combatants (including nuclear and conventional missile-capable submarines and destroyers) and auxiliaries were making use of the port. By the mid-1980s, surveillance aircraft and medium-range bombers were based at Cam Ranh, protected by a complement of MiG-23 Floggers that are capable of speeds up to Mach 2.3 (almost two and a half times the speed of sound), have a combat radius of about 1,150 kilometers, and are armed with at least six air-to-air missiles—all of which makes them formidable air-combat aircraft.

In a time of conflict, the armed forces of the industrialized democracies would inevitably take steps to neutralize the effectiveness of the Soviet base at Cam Ranh Bay. Nevertheless, the presence of substantial Soviet air and naval forces near the major chokepoints in the sea lanes of communication in Southeast Asia, through which the bulk of the traffic to Northeast Asia must pass, is a matter of considerable strategic importance. It complicates U.S. military planning and obviously influences the diplomatic and political considerations of all the nations in the region. For the first time since the Second World War, the whole of Southeast Asia is exposed to a threatening military presence capable of interdicting the major sea lanes so essential to the defense of the West Pacific.

Events of the past two decades have reminded Americans once again of the political and diplomatic importance of military power quite apart from its use in a general conflict. A strong nation uses its armed forces, particularly its naval forces, to influence the course of events in peacetime. It also uses them in a variety of "low-intensity" engagements, ranging from a reaction to terrorist activities to a response to local and regional warfare. More important, perhaps, is that a credible deterrent capability reduces the possibility of war, maintains the confidence of allies, and enhances the nation's political effectiveness.

The U.S. deterrent capability in Southeast Asia, as we shall see, depends substantially on access to bases in the Philippines. The political and economic situation in the Philippine Republic therefore has serious implications for the U.S. military presence in the region.

## Developments in the Philippines

Between 1965 and the early 1980s—while the Soviet Union was building its military power and its forward-projection capability—certain developments in the Philippines negatively affected the U.S. position. For reasons having little if anything to do with the U.S. military presence, the Philippines gradually lapsed into crisis.

The Philippine Republic has since its beginning charted an unsteady course of economic and political modernization. Between 1946 and the beginning of the 1970s it made considerable progress.[30] Nonetheless, by 1972, the end of President Ferdinand Marcos's second term, a Communist insurgency in the countryside on Luzon (Luzon and Mindanao are the two largest islands in the chain), a Muslim separatist rebellion on Mindanao, and an increasing number of political murders throughout the country provided the constitutional basis for a presidential declaration of martial law.[31] With martial law came the inevitable derogation of civil and political rights, and some of the enemies of the regime fled to the United States to begin an organized opposition.

In the Philippines the anti-Marcos opposition organized itself around a number of issues, one of which was the U.S. military presence. As we have seen, a vocal minority had long been opposed to the U.S. military bases, but the political crisis brought on by the declaration of martial law galvanized those opponents. Former senators Lorenzo Tañada and Jose Diokno, for example, became aggressive spokesmen for the anti-Marcos opposition. Some who had opposed Marcos on other grounds ultimately chose to oppose him on the issue of the American military presence. Political leaders such as Alejandro Lichauco,[32] who had expressed objection to the U.S.-Philippine security connection before the advent of martial law, subsequently used the issue to defame Marcos as a "lackey of American imperialism."[33]

Because Marcos remained a staunch advocate of the U.S.-Philippine security arrangements, most of his opposition came to assume a position critical of the American military presence. Gradually, the opposition to the bases agreement broadened into an entire catalog of objections to U.S. activities in the islands. The security relationship came to be seen as only part of a complex system in which the United States had subjected the Philippines to "exploitive victimization" for more than half a century. Almost every disability that afflicted the archipelago was blamed on the "international capitalism" that emanated from North America. Former senator Lorenzo Tañada, who would later serve as advisor to the successor to Marcos, insisted that the United States maintained the bases solely as a means of oppressing the Philippine people.[34] In the view of former senator Jose Diokno, too, the bases served only to perpetuate Philippine dependency and U.S. economic exploitation.[35]

Tañada and Diokno were among the most prominent leaders of the "moderate opposition. Other leaders from a variety of groups took similar stands. By the summer of 1983, the major organization of the non-Communist opposition to Marcos, the United Nationalist Democratic Organization (UNIDO), had made objection to the Military Bases Agreement a formal plank in its program. In May 1983, former senator Salvador Laurel, titular head of UNIDO, announced that he was committed to abrogation of the agreement.[36]

In December 1984, Corazon Aquino, the widow of the assassinated former senator Benigno Aquino, put together a "statement of principles" designed to unify all the anti-Marcos moderates. The resulting "principles of unity" included the commitment that "foreign military bases on Philippine territory must be removed and no foreign military bases shall hereafter be allowed."[37] Almost all members of the opposition signed the unity program.

Therefore when Corazon Aquino acceded to power in Manila in February 1986, many in her entourage were opposed to the U.S. military presence as a matter of principle. What had been little more than a minority view was now a central conviction of a substantial number of people who were preparing to assume control of the Philippine political system.

To assess what that means for U.S. interests, the interests of the people of the Philippines, and the interests of the non-Communist nations of the world, we must examine the nature and function of the U.S. military bases in the Philippines.

# 2

# The U.S. Pacific Presence

**D**ISCUSSION OF THE U.S. military installations in the Philippines usually focuses on their role in deterring a Soviet adventure in the South China Sea or the Indian Ocean, or their function in actual conflict with the Soviet Union. Certainly the deterrent role looms large, and it is the one we shall examine first. But, as we shall see, the security function of the bases extends considerably beyond that.

In early 1980, Admiral Robert L. J. Long, then commander in chief of the U.S. Pacific Command, testified in a congressional hearing that U.S. ground, air, and naval forces under his operational command could not guarantee success should a direct engagement with the Soviet Union erupt. The Soviet military buildup in the Pacific since the 1970s, he said, made the situation "too close to call." The Soviet military presence in East Asia now involves fully one-third of the Soviet Union's entire conventional and nuclear inventory.

The buildup took place in two phases. Between the mid-1960s and 1978 Moscow doubled its mobile infantry forces in Northeast Asia, from 210,000 to about 410,000 effectives. The number of divisions grew from about twenty-five to forty-three. The communications and transportation infrastructure was strengthened, and command, control, and supply facilities were hardened against conventional and nuclear blast effects. Combat aircraft available were increased by about 35 per cent. Major combatants in the Soviet Pacific Fleet increased by a relatively modest 10 per cent, and the number of ballistic missile submarines went from ten to thirty.

All this accelerated in 1978, when Moscow established a Far Eastern High Command with command and control properties the same as those in the Warsaw Pact region of Eastern Europe.

Soviet forces developed the same capability to conduct large-scale military operations in Asia that they had in Eastern Europe.

Also in 1978, Vietnam joined the Communist nations' Council for Economic and Mutual Assistance (CEMA) and signed a treaty of friendship with the Soviet Union. Having thereby gained access to the onshore facilities of Cam Ranh Bay, Soviet armed forces soon occupied Afghanistan. This brought them within striking range of the critical Middle Eastern waterways over which passes one-third of all U.S. trade and most of the cargo and tanker traffic supplying the non-Communist countries of East, Southeast, and Northeast Asia.

Since 1978 the Soviet Union has emphasized power-projection forces in Asia. In the past, the weapon systems of the Soviet forces in East Asia lagged about a decade behind those in the western USSR and the Warsaw Pact. After 1978, that was no longer true. The Soviet SS-20 intermediate-range missiles that became operational in 1977 were emplaced in East Asia less than a year later. By the mid-1980s, fully one-third of the total SS-20 forces available (about 165 missiles) were based in Soviet East Asia. In 1978 the first Backfire bombers made their appearance there. MiG-25 Foxbat and MiG-31 Foxhound interceptors, among the most modern in the Soviet inventory, now provide frontline air defense assets in East Asia, and the newest longer-range SU-24 Fencers provide extended reach for combat well beyond the Soviet borders.

## The Soviet Naval Presence

For our purposes, the most important development has been at sea: the transformation of the Soviet Pacific Fleet from a relatively modest coastal defense force into the largest of the four Soviet fleets, with more than 800 ships and submarines in service.[1] Its major surface combatants now number about eighty-seven and include two of the Soviets' four operational aircraft carriers. On any given day about sixty Soviet vessels can be found operating along the sea lanes that stretch from the Middle East through the Indian Ocean to the South China Sea.

The number of out-of-area Soviet naval ship days has more than doubled since 1978—a clear indicator of forward deployment and power projection.

The Soviet presence at Cam Ranh is particularly significant. Since 1979, Soviet military aid to Vietnam has totaled more than $5 billion—evidence of the importance Moscow assigns to the facilities there. Before 1978, Soviet naval units operated only episodically in the South China Sea. Cam Ranh was used only for contingency support, emergency ship repair, and occasionally shelter for auxiliary vessels. By the mid-1980s, however, Cam Ranh had become a major staging complex for Soviet Pacific Fleet vessels, submarines, and aircraft outside Soviet Northeast Asia.

The base is undergoing further development. Floating piers increase berthing space, and improved underground petroleum-storage facilities are almost completed. The base now provides afloat support facilities for submarines and surface ships as well as airfield support facilities for Soviet fighter and bomber aircraft.

The base access in Vietnam improves the response time, range, and duration of Soviet surveillance of shipping and Western naval operations along the major sea routes in Southeast Asia. It improves the flexibility of Soviet operations and permits the rapid augmentation of Soviet forces along the Indian Ocean and Middle Eastern sea lanes of communication.

In spring 1984, Soviet and Vietnamese forces conducted a major joint naval exercise in the South China Sea. The Kiev class aircraft carrier *Minsk* and an Ivan Rogov class amphibious assault-and-landing vessel participated. After complex maneuvers at sea, the exercise concluded with an amphibious landing on the Vietnamese coast—the first demonstration of Soviet joint-operations power-projection capabilities in the South China Sea and of Moscow's determination to conduct complex naval operations far beyond its home waters.

The Soviet air and naval presence in South Vietnam gives the USSR reconnaissance coverage of the entire sea route from Aden (on the Arabian Peninsula) to Vladivostok, anti-submarine patrol surveillance from Hokkaido to Sri Lanka, and anti-ship missile coverage from Petropavlovsk (on Kamchatka Peninsula in the northern Pacific) to Perth. The Soviet units in Vietnam are outside the geographic barriers and constraints that inhibit Soviet naval operations from home ports in Northeast Asia. They are the functional counterpart of the U.S. Seventh Fleet forward deployed forces.

Clearly, Moscow is committed to improving its ability to interdict the major sea lanes of communication in the Indian Ocean and the South China Sea should circumstances so require. This capability has considerable diplomatic and political significance.[2]

### The Philippine Counterweight

Against this growing presence in the South China Sea, the U.S. military facilities in the Philippines serve as a counterweight. Clark Air Field and the naval base at Subic Bay are clearly the centerpieces of U.S. defensive and deterrent strategy in the region.[3] Clark is the only major U.S. tactical air force installation in the West Pacific outside Japan and Korea. It is the home base for the Thirteenth Tactical Air Force, charged not only with the air defense of the Philippines and the entire region stretching northward to South Korea but also with the projection of U.S. power across the Indian Ocean as far as eastern Africa. Clark Field is the air logistics hub for all U.S. forces in the West Pacific and provides major aircraft maintenance facilities and large stockpiles of fuel, ammunition, and other military supplies. It has the greatest capacity for airlift of personnel and supplies in the West Pacific.

At Subic Bay, the U.S. Seventh Fleet deploys about thirty-four major surface combatants, including two formidable aircraft carrier battle groups, six submarines, and seven amphibious assault ships, supported by a substantial logistics train and accorded air cover by nearly 200 combat aircraft. These forces have as their mission the suppression of Soviet aircraft and submarines that would threaten the air and sea routes. They would also serve to interdict the Soviets' supply lines to their Vietnamese bases from Siberia and the Indian Ocean, and to their forces in the northeast. The Philippine bases would facilitate such operations because of their proximity to the sea and air routes that pass through and over the chokepoints in the Indonesian straits, across the South China Sea, and east of the Philippines. The Philippine bases are also within effective tactical range of the Soviet bases in Vietnam.[4] With substantial U.S. naval and air forces present in the Philippines, Moscow could not count on the protracted use of its bases in Vietnam in time of conflict.

The U.S. forces in the Philippines, along with those based in Japan, Guam, and Hawaii, would be used not only to neutralize Soviet forces in Vietnam but also to give the United States the capacity to conduct military operations in the South China Sea, the Indian Ocean, and the Persian Gulf. U.S. strategy for Persian Gulf security depends heavily on sustaining the sea and air routes through the West Pacific and Southeast Asia. The Soviet sea route to East Africa and the Persian Gulf from its Pacific Fleet bases traverses the passages in Southeast Asia. Any Soviet military operations in those regions, other than a border crossing into Iran or Pakistan, would have to be supported by sea. Soviet forces seeking access to the Persian Gulf from the Pacific would be intercepted by U.S. forces based in the Philippines.[5]

The airlift of U.S. troops bound for the Persian Gulf region would use Clark Field as a major transit point. U.S. strategic planning calls for equipment and ordnance prepositioned at the Indian Ocean island of Diego Garcia to be supplied to combat troops airlifted from the United States via Clark. Alternative routing, not using Clark, would take longer, require more airlift assets, and necessitate the (perhaps reluctant) assistance of allied powers.[6]

Very few defense analysts would minimize the importance of the U.S. military installations in the Philippines either in a general conflict—whether below or above the nuclear threshold—or in local conflicts conducted by proxies or the major powers themselves. It is evident that the Soviet presence in Southeast Asia is a latent threat to all the non-Communist states of the region. It heartens the aggressive intentions of Hanoi.

And it is the most recent evidence of Moscow's decision to project its power everywhere in the world. For the United States to fail to counter Soviet moves would signal a manifest failure of resolve and could have grave consequences for the interests of democratic nations everywhere.

### Other Purposes of the U.S. Presence

Southeast Asia and the South China Sea are very singular parts of the world, and the U.S. military presence in the region serves other purposes than as a counterweight to the Soviet Union. Perhaps no single issue better captures the complexity of the security environment than the conflicting territorial and seabed claims that characterize the region. The result of a variety of influences, some dating back into the early history of the area, these jurisdictional disputes could lead to overt conflict, with fateful consequences for international peace.

The South China Sea, roughly the size of the Mediterranean, is bordered on the west by peninsular Southeast Asia and elsewhere by an arc of islands that stretches from the Taiwan Strait in the north to the Malacca Strait in the southwest. The waters of the sea itself are dotted with about 125 small islands, cays, atolls, reefs, sandbars, shoals, and lagoons. Most of the land fragments are uninhabitable.

There are two relatively large groups of coral islands: the Paracel Islands (Hsisha) and the Spratly Group (Nansha). The Paracels are an archipelagic complex of some fifteen islets and about a dozen reefs and shoals. The Spratlys are a widely scattered collection of shoals, reefs, rocks, and islets that stretch over 600 miles of the South China Sea from southeast to northwest. Northeast of the Spratlys and the Paracels is Pratas Island (Tungsha); nearly five miles long and one mile wide, it is one of the largest islands in the region.

This is the cluttered sea that virtually all surface traffic from Europe and the Middle East must traverse to reach Japan and the newly industrialized market economies of Northeast and East Asia. Most of the tanker and dry cargo carriers serving East and Northeast Asia enter the South China Sea through the

Strait of Malacca and exit through the Taiwan Strait or the Bashi Channel (between Taiwan and the Philippines). Only the largest tankers, which cannot navigate these shallow straits, use alternate routes.

Most of the shipping lanes in the South China Sea pass near the islands, atolls, and banks that dot the region. Occupation and control of such territory could entail influence over the flow of traffic. For at least that reason the territorial fragments are of lasting interest to the principal actors in the area.

### Territorial Claims in the Sea

At least two of these major actors, the Soviet Union and the People's Republic of China, have direct interests involved in the territorial and subsea claims made in the South China Sea. Beyond that, almost every country in the region has made formal or informal claims to territories or over the continental shelf in the Southeast Asian interocean basin.[7]

Between the two world wars, France, China, and Japan all laid claim to the islands of the region. After the war Japan forfeited all claims, and France transferred its disputed title to Vietnam. Both the People's Republic of China and the Republic of China on Taiwan claim all the islands as the successors to the Qing Dynasty, which held historic claim over the entire sea. By the early 1970s, all the claimants had garrisoned islands. The PRC maintains a marine garrison on Woody Island in the Paracels. The Nationalist Chinese maintain a force on Pratas Island and on Itu Aba Island in the Spratly archipelago. Vietnamese forces maintain a military presence on Spratly Island itself.

In 1956 several enterprising Filipinos took "formal possession" of five unoccupied islets in the Spratly group "by right of discovery." Since that time, Manila has announced that some fifty-three islets, rocks, and atolls, collectively identified as "Kalayaan," have become an administrative district of Palawan Province in the Republic of the Philippines—protected by a marine contingent and attack units of the Philippine air force. As recently as April 1983, Cesar Virata, then prime minister of the Philippines, warned all claimants to the territory in the South

China Sea that any attempt to reclaim the Kalayaan Islands would be "considered an assault against the Republic of the Philippines" and would receive appropriate rebuff.[8]

By the early 1970s, then, there were four major claimants to the territories scattered throughout the South China Sea. Changes wrought in the international law of the sea after 1945 were creating further complexity, and by the early 1980s the entire region was gridlocked with claims and counterclaims that involved not only the territories but the adjacent continental shelves, the subjacent waters, and the seabed and subseabed resources as well.

### The Changing Law of the Sea

With the end of World War Two in the Pacific, all the former colonial dependencies in Southeast Asia attained their independence. The appearance of these new states created more claimants in the contest for territorial and economic exploitation rights in the South China Sea. Movement in that direction was reinforced by profound changes in what had been traditional practice in the international law of the sea. As a result of these changes, the nature of a sovereign coastal state's control of its territorial and adjacent waters and subsea land extension, as well as the ownership and control of islands, was transformed.[9]

That transformation began with the proclamation by President Harry S Truman in 1945 that the United States was prepared to assert "jurisdiction and control" over the natural resources associated with its adjacent subsea "continental shelf." So novel was this concept that in the formal proclamation of the claim no allusion was made to any established legal precedents. The idea seems to have evolved out of practical economic considerations.[10]

The contention that a state could extend its effective control beyond its immediate "territorial waters" (which traditionally had meant three miles offshore) to include the subsea prolongation of the shore brought a number of consequences. Although it was not immediately clear what a "continental shelf" was, and how far it might extend beyond traditional territorial waters, such control obviously could involve substantial economic benefits. Coastal states therefore initiated a spate of claims of exclusive rights to the living resources of the waters above the continental shelves, or to the living and nonliving resources of the offshore seabeds.

The first United Nations Conference on the Law of the Sea was convened at Geneva in 1958. From this emerged the Convention on the Continental Shelf, which sought to regularize what was becoming an almost universal practice of coastal states to make ill-defined, sometimes conflicting, and almost always exclusive claims on offshore sea and seabed resources.[11]

As international jurists grappled with these issues, it became clear that the extended concept of jurisdiction would inevitably involve judgments about islands and their subsea extensions. If coastal states could extend their control to offshore continental shelves, island states clearly could claim the same rights. And if island *states* could claim such rights, what rights attended the island *possessions* of sovereign states?

## The Jumble of Claims

The peninsular and insular states of Southeast Asia have now made claim to jurisdiction and control over their continental shelves. Those claims create complex jurisdictional problems— a complexity greatly enhanced by the fact that each of the island and atoll fragments in the region can generate its own jurisdictional claim to the continental shelf.

Both the Philippines and Indonesia have passed laws that provide the foundation for extensive offshore jurisdiction ranging over territorial waters, an exclusive economic zone, and supplementary control over seabed resources beyond that. These claims bring them into conflict with other states' claims.

In the eastern reaches of the South China Sea, both the Nationalist and the Communist Chinese claim Nanyen Rock—a fragment barely above water off the Philippine island of Luzon. The current disposition of the Philippine government is to claim jurisdiction over an economic zone 200 miles offshore of Luzon, and so its seabed claim conflicts with those of both Chinese claimants. Moreover, Manila has used its territorial claims in the Spratlys (claimed by the PRC, the ROC, and Vietnam) as the basis for its seabed exploration and exploitation off the Reed Bank—claimed by both the PRC and the ROC.[12]

Indonesia's offshore claims bring Jakarta into potential conflict with the People's Republic of China. The PRC claims not only the Spratly Islands but the James Shoal, which lies directly off Sarawak near the large Indonesian island of Natuna. The territory off Sarawak and Natuna is an area of intense oil exploration, and the conflicting claims cause considerable concern.

Malaysia and Thailand, too, have proclaimed exclusive economic rights to their offshore shelves. This brings Malaysia into potential conflict not only with Indonesia but with the PRC as well.[13]

The PRC's claim to "inalienable sovereignty" over the islands of the South China Sea involves shelf entitlements that conflict with the exclusive economic rights claimed by the Socialist Republic of Vietnam, Thailand, Malaysia, Indonesia, and the Philippines—and perhaps Brunei and Singapore as well. In 1974, representatives at the Colombo conference on economic rights maintained that "China hereby reiterates that all seabed resources in Chinese coastal sea areas and those off her islands belong to China. China alone has the right to prospect and exploit those seabed resources."[14]

Under current international practice, it is not clear to what extent a continental state that owns an island in the high seas gains exclusive rights to the resources of its surrounding continental shelf. Earlier, the consensus appeared to be that an island could generate its own exclusive economic zone on the continental shelf. In theory, that would allow any island, no matter how small, to claim such rights.[15] The troubling implications of shelf entitlement for islands have led to various attempts at restriction. Recently, for example, shelf rights have been denied "rocks which cannot sustain human habitation or economic life of their own."[16]

But these restrictions seem to have had little effect on the nature of the claims to territories in the South China Sea. The states involved appear to believe that the islands, shoals, and atolls can support claims to the adjacent continental shelf. The authorities in Beijing, for example, have insisted that islands and archipelagos be accorded the same shelf entitlements as continental states.[17]

A number of studies, supported by seismic and geological surveys, have suggested that the East China and South China seas may be rich in recoverable oil deposits.[18] By 1982, over 300 promising areas of the seabed had been identified. The assumed amount of recoverable oil varies from Soviet estimates of 11 billion barrels to the PRC's own estimate of almost 160 billion barrels. Beijing anticipates that by 1990 offshore oil reserves would provide it with enough foreign exchange to fund about 23 per cent of all its projected imports.[19]

By the mid-1980s, almost every state around the South China Sea had extended a claim into the interocean basin, and nearly every claim conflicted with one lodged by another state.[20] The most persistent claims are those of the Socialist Republic of Vietnam and the People's Republic of China.

### The PRC and the Use of Force

As the issues of territorial, maritime, and seabed claims in the South China Sea have become more complex, the potential for overt conflict has increased. The claims made by Vietnam are supported by the Soviet Union. The People's Republic of China has made it eminently clear that it is prepared to use military force to protect its claims, and its military power is extending farther and farther into the region. All the states of the area find themselves drawn into a protracted conflict that could easily explode into violence. Each member of the Association of Southeast Asian Nations (ASEAN)—Brunei, Indonesia, Malaysia, the Philippines, Singapore, and Thailand—has expressed concern over the potential for violence in the region.

Beijing introduced military force into this volatile environment in 1974, in an attempt to solve its territorial dispute with Vietnam over the Paracels. At the time, Beijing was negotiating with the United States for "normalized" diplomatic relations, and everyone assumed that the Chinese leaders were concerned with projecting an image of international responsibility. The PRC had not used armed force to settle a territorial dispute since the Sino-Indian War of 1962. It had not used a combined amphibious assault against an opponent since 1958—when its behavior brought it to the brink of conflict with the United States in the Taiwan Strait. Few specialists expected an armed attack.

But in January 1974 the armed forces of the PRC embarked on an amphibious assault against the Paracel archipelago and, in short but decisive air and naval engagements with South Vietnamese forces stationed there, seized control. Since then, the PRC has continued to insist upon all its claims in the region and has shown an increased capacity and determination to project its power into the South China Sea.

Since the early 1970s Beijing has systematically worked to develop blue-water capability for its naval forces, previously little more than a coastal defense force. By 1980, the PRC Navy was displaying some rather sophisticated capabilities. At that time a task force of eighteen vessels from its three fleets succeeded in retrieving a reentry vehicle that had been carried by an intercontinental ballistic missile to a splashdown site 4,000 miles away from the nearest Chinese port. In the course of the operation, Chinese personnel used helicopters operating from pads on submarine rescue vessels. In effect, the PRC Navy now has the rudiments of the capabilities required for out-of-area deployment.[21]

### The Continuing PRC-Vietnam Conflict

In May 1984 a naval squadron from the PRC conducted exercises near islands in the Spratlys occupied by Vietnam.[22] At almost precisely the same moment, the Sixth National People's Congress in Beijing was recommending that the Spratlys be incorporated into the administrative infrastructure of Hainan Island, a large island off the PRC's southwest coast. The improved forward-projection capabilities of the PRC Navy were therefore joined by what appears to be a formidable political determination.

As the PRC has developed these capabilities, its hostile contacts with military forces from Vietnam have increased. In March 1982, Vietnamese and PRC naval vessels exchanged fire.[23] Vietnam, which is seeking increasingly to develop its own offshore oil recovery, appears prepared to challenge the PRC's claims throughout the South China Sea. Hanoi has announced its decision to "consolidate the Spratly archipelago" and associated territories "into a stalwart steel fortress to defend the fatherland's sovereignty" against the growing threat from the PRC.[24]

In response, the PRC has enhanced its military facilities in the Paracels. It has built several harbors and a naval base to service vessels as large as frigates. The base on Woody Island could be used as a staging area for a campaign against the Spratlys.

Hanoi, in turn, has added missile-capable Petya class frigates to its naval array, hardened its emplacements in the Spratlys, and constructed an airstrip in the islands to service Soviet-supplied Su-17s and MiG-23s that could provide suitable air cover in the event of conflict. Amboyna Cay in the Spratlys is now garrisoned by about 150 regular Vietnamese troops in what is apparently part of a general program of force enhancement in the archipelago.[25] That Vietnam is serious about its claims to the continental shelf, and about sovereignty over the islands in the South China Sea, is evidenced by the fact that Hanoi twice risked a major confrontation: it fired on Western-owned supply vessels in the Gulf of Tonkin in July 1979, and, as mentioned above, it engaged naval vessels from the PRC in an exchange of gunfire in March 1982. In June 1983 a Vietnamese gunboat forced a French-operated drilling rig to vacate contested waters in the Gulf of Tonkin.[26]

### The Oil Incentive

To complicate matters further, Malaysia has sent its commandos to occupy the island of Terumba Layang Layanag in the Spratlys. Using its own interpretation of its continental shelf entitlements, Kuala Lumpur is apparently concerned about protecting its critical offshore oil and natural gas industries.[27]

Petroleum and natural gas products make up about 27 per cent of Malaysia's current exports, and most of its recoverable reserves are offshore on its continental shelf.

The search for offshore oil is one of the principal incentives for competition in the South China Sea. Petroleum exports now constitute the major portion of the exports of Indonesia (70 per cent) and Brunei (99 per cent). Both Thailand and the Philippines are developing offshore fields; Manila is exploiting at least two commercially productive fields off the Reed Bank.

Given the projected growth rates of the economies of the region and their foreign exchange problems, it is clear that the ASEAN states have every incentive to exploit recoverable oil deposits. Offshore economic zones, even if they are currently nonproductive, must be secured to accommodate further growth and anticipated technological development.

## The Potential for Violence

Clearly, the behavior of the actors in the region will reflect several factors—including the prevailing price of oil, the support provided by security partners, and changes in international practice concerning continental shelf entitlements and island rights. Another influential factor is the military capabilities of the various claimants. It is generally accepted, for example, that the PRC would also have attacked the Spratlys when it attacked the Paracels in 1974 if its armed forces had had the capability.[28] At that time, its aircraft from Hainan Island could not provide the air cover required for a combined assault against the Spratlys; their combat range restricted their operations to the Paracels.

Since then, the PRC's armed forces have been appreciably modernized and the endurance and firepower of its naval vessels enhanced. In May 1984, Beijing demonstrated its enhanced capabilities by dispatching a naval squadron composed of two frigates, a troop ship, and a support vessel to circumnavigate the Spratly archipelago. The assault troops offlanded on Hainan could have been used for an amphibious attack on the Spratlys.

In response, Hanoi has expanded the forward-projection capacity of its armed forces. In the 1984 joint naval exercises mentioned previously, the Vietnamese demonstrated rather sophisticated capabilities by staging a joint amphibious operation with the Soviet Union involving landing craft and frigates. The Soviet Navy supplied a large amphibious assault ship, the *Aleksandr Nikoleyev,* and the Soviet light aircraft carrier *Minsk* provided the potential for accompanying air cover. Major Soviet naval combatants now constitute a permanent presence in the South China Sea, and Vietnam's future behavior in the region will be significantly influenced by how far Moscow decides it will go to support Hanoi's territorial and maritime claims.

The potential for unintended violence is high. Elements from the armed forces of most of the claimants to shelf entitlements and territory in the South China Sea are scattered throughout the region. Combatants from the People's Republic of China, the Republic of China on Taiwan, the Socialist Republic of Vietnam, the Philippines, Malaysia, and Indonesia remain permanently on station on the contested islands or on immediately adjacent islands. Military aircraft from the Soviet Union, the Socialist Republic of Vietnam, the Philippines, Malaysia, and Indonesia undertake missions in overlapping airspace, increasing the risk of inadvertent and potentially hostile contact.

Into this conflict environment the United States introduces a significant measure of stability. With U.S. naval forces stationed in the immediate vicinity, any disposition toward violence in the area is inhibited. It is very unlikely that any party to the conflicts in the South China Sea would venture on a military solution to its territorial disputes if the U.S. response time were short and its available force formidable.

In 1974, when the Communist Chinese decided to attack the Paracel Islands, they did so only with the conviction that the U.S. Seventh Fleet was fully involved in the denouement in Vietnam and could contribute little to the risks to which the PRC forces would be exposed. Had there been a U.S. naval and air presence in the area, it is at least doubtful that Beijing would have embarked on its aggression.

Given these considerations, most of the states in the region advocate a continued U.S. military presence. The U.S. forces, representing a major power with no immediate stake in the territorial disputes of the area, are considered a stabilizing factor. Whether to offset growing Soviet capabilities in the region, or to reduce the prospects of misadventure growing out of territorial disputes, the U.S. military presence in Southeast Asia has been welcomed by all the nations of ASEAN and is actively supported by Australia.[29]

Central to that presence are the U.S. military facilities in the Philippines. These have increased in strategic and regional importance over the past several decades and are now a critical component of U.S. foreign policy in one of the most important areas of the world.

# 3

# *The U.S. Base Facilities*

THE MISSIONS ASSIGNED to the United States armed forces stationed in the Philippine archipelago are complex and demanding. Those forces are charged with protecting U.S. security interests in the entire West Pacific, interests that include the defense of our treaty allies in either a general or a local conflict involving either a major or any regional power. The U.S. forces are designed to provide a credible deterrent against the expanding capabilities of the Soviet Union, a fighting force in the event of general conflict, and both a deterrent to local conflict and, should deterrence fail, an influential fighting force in such a conflict. The U.S. military presence complicates the planning of any actor in the region—the more credible the presence, the more complicated the planning. And as a major military power in the region with no immediate interest in most local disputes, the United States can effectively serve as mediator, thereby reducing the probability of regional violence.

All these responsibilities are translated into missions assigned to the U.S. Seventh Fleet and Thirteenth Air Force and discharged from bases in the Philippines. As the missions have become more demanding, the base facilities have grown more complex. The major facilities that service the Seventh Fleet and Thirteenth Air Force are the Subic Bay/Cubi Point naval and air complex and Clark Air Base. These are supplemented by small facilities elsewhere on Luzon: John Hay Air Station in Baguio City, the Naval Radio Station at Capas (actually part of the Clark reservation), the U.S. Naval Communications Station at San Miguel (technically part of the Subic Bay/Cubi Point complex), and the Wallace Air Station at Poro Point.

## SUBIC NAVAL BASE AND CUBI POINT

The Seventh Fleet consists of two carrier battle groups, associated surface combatants, submarines, one Marine amphibious
unit, and one Marine battalion landing team. Its headquarters,
the Subic Bay/Cubi Point complex, is located in a deep-water
harbor formed by volcanic activity about fifty miles northwest of
Manila. The protected harbors and tropical climate make Subic
an ideal location for ship services and support. The base is the
primary staging area for all U.S. naval activities in Southeast
Asian waters. Located between the Pacific and Indian oceans, it
is ideally suited for logistical, command, control, communications, and training functions.

The Subic Bay and Cubi Point facilities occupy approximately
62,000 acres and together constitute one of the largest naval
bases in the world. Subic's three major wharves have a total
length of 6,000 feet, with berthing space at depths ranging from
twenty to forty feet—depths that can accommodate the largest
aircraft carriers in the U.S. Navy. The installations at Subic Bay
and Cubi Point are estimated to be worth $1.2 billion, exclusive
of land value. The complex includes the Naval Station at Port
Olangpo and the Naval Magazine at Camayan Point.

In accordance with the 1979 revision of the U.S.-Philippine
Bases Agreement, Subic Naval Base has a Philippine commander and a subordinate U.S. facility commander who is
directly responsible for the day-to-day operations of the U.S.
military on the 20,000 acres that compose the actual U.S.
facility. The facility commander supervises approximately 9,000
U.S. sailors, about 3,500–4,000 of them stationed at the base
and the rest attached to ships berthed there. The U.S. Department of Defense has about 560 civilian employees at Subic Bay/
Cubi Point along with some 23,000 Philippine workers.[1]

### Ship Support Services

The superb deep-water bay on which the complex is located
faces the South China Sea and is well stationed for rapid

projection of naval power or the support of vessels operating in the Indian Ocean. When in 1979 and 1980 developments in Iran and Afghanistan made force deployments prudent, carrier task forces were dispatched from Subic Bay to the Indian Ocean. Those operations required almost continuous resupply. Logistics operations were conducted out of the Philippine bases.

The U.S. decision to develop facilities at Diego Garcia (in the Chagos Archipelago) and elsewhere in the Indian Ocean requires that a train of supply and replenishment vessels be operated out of Subic Bay. The storage facilities on the islands in the Indian Ocean cannot hold supplies, arms, or fuel for more than thirty days of operation. To maintain the U.S. presence at the current level without the Philippine facilities would require a substantial increase in naval support and replenishment ships— transporting materiel much greater distances at much greater expense.

The supply and logistical tasks at Subic Bay are performed by the Naval Supply Depot and the Naval Magazine, which store, service, and distribute supplies and ordnance to all units of the Seventh Fleet. From its 1.75 million square feet of storage space, the Naval Supply Depot issues over $13.5 million worth of supplies monthly. It maintains an inventory of over 180,000 items and handles over 4 million barrels of fuel a month, out of a storage capacity of more than 110 million gallons of petroleum, oil, and lubricants.[2] The depot's twenty-two mammoth tanks make it the largest facility of its kind in the world.

The Naval Magazine stores about $300 million worth of ammunition in 3.8 million cubic feet of storage. Nine buildings and an ammunition wharf have an estimated value of about $30 million. The magazine processes about 25,000 tons of ammunition a month and can supply the needs of all major combatant vessels of the Seventh Fleet.

Subic Bay's capabilities are supplemented by a 200-bed Regional Medical Center that provides modern care. Over 850,000 kilowatt hours of electricity are produced on this facility each day. The medical center could deal effectively with a rapid increase in population as well as an influx of battle casualties.

## Ship Repair Services

In addition to these support functions, Subic Bay provides major repair facilities for large vessels that are unavailable elsewhere in the West Pacific. The repair operations are housed in over 800,000 square feet of building space. Three wharves enclose the area and are serviced by portal and floating cranes. Four floating dry docks can handle vessels displacing up to 54,000 tons. During the Vietnam conflict, the repair facilities handled as many as 110 ships at a time, berthing vessels three deep at the principal wharves. At present, nearly 60 per cent of all repair and servicing for the U.S. Seventh Fleet is done at Subic Bay.[3] The skilled labor is performed by 4,000 Filipinos, whose wage scale is about one-seventh that of comparable workers in the United States.[4]

Without the Subic Bay facilities, larger U.S. warships needing repair would have to travel to Yokosuka in Japan, which is about three days' steaming time from Subic. The consequences would of course be a lengthened turnaround time and a reduced number of ship days on station.

In short, Subic Bay has everything a naval force could require: a fine deep-water harbor, extensive storage structures, elaborate repair facilities serviced by a skilled and cost-efficient labor force, and, as we shall see, several nearby air bases that enhance its multi-mission capabilities.[5] Its range of services is not available to the United States anywhere else in the Southwest Pacific.

## The Cubi Point Airfield

The airfield at nearby Cubi Point can accommodate as many as 200 aircraft at a time and provides service and support for several major air squadrons and U.S. Navy and Marine Corps flying units. Each month the field averages 17,000 takeoffs and landings, the transit of more than 3,500 passengers, and approximately 800 tons of military airlift. Cubi Point airfield serves as the primary operational site for the aircraft carriers of the Seventh Fleet, providing dockside parking for their entire aircraft complement.[6]

It also serves as a base for P-3 Orion anti-submarine-warfare aircraft, which have a range of 1,000 nautical miles and can remain on station in the air for seven hours. The Orions are charged with surveillance of the West Pacific and Indian Ocean. They track submarines in the entire region and provide early-warning intelligence to base communications units. Some ten A-4 Skyhawk light-attack bombers are stationed at Cubi Point. The airfield maintains aircraft for delivery onto carriers, and provides a transit point for aircraft enroute to other stations. The Naval Patrol Wing at Cubi Point undertakes target-towing for surface and airborne gunnery practice.

Cubi Point has traffic controllers, air-sea rescue personnel, and fire and crash crews as well as service personnel for aircraft and weaponry. About 900 U.S. military personnel are stationed at the airfield, which also employs nearly 500 Filipinos. Cubi Point houses 3,500 military and more than 700 foreign personnel and could expand rapidly if required.

The Subic Bay/Cubi Point complex has no counterpart in the Southwest Pacific. Without it, the U.S. forward-deployment and power-projection capabilities would be significantly impaired.

## CLARK AIR BASE

Thirty-five miles northeast of Subic Bay is Clark Air Base, headquarters of the Thirteenth Air Force. It is the largest U.S. military facility outside the continental United States.[7] About four dozen F-4 Phantom fighters are permanently assigned to Clark as the Third Tactical Fighter Wing of the Thirteenth Air Force. They are supplemented by about a dozen F-5E Tigers used in combat training. An airlift component is provided by some sixteen C-130 Hercules transports of the 374th Tactical Airlift Wing. Clark Air Base provides facilities for a variety of other support aircraft and helicopters as well. Besides the aircraft permanently assigned to bases in the Philippines, each carrier berthed at those bases has a shipboard complement of seventy-five to ninety combat aircraft.

The reservation on which Clark Air Base is located covers

about 131,000 acres, of which some 9,000 acres—about 8 per cent—is used for the runway, terminal, storage and repair structures, offices, barracks, and housing (a total of about 2,700 separate buildings). Through the 1979 emendations to the U.S.-Philippines Military Bases Agreement, the portion of the reservation not used directly as the U.S. facility—that is, 92 per cent—has reverted to Philippine control. With the permission of the government in Manila, U.S. forces also use part of 46,000-acre Crow Valley as a target range for gunnery and aerial bombardment practice.

The entire Clark reservation has a Philippine base commander. A U.S. commander serves as executive officer for the U.S. facilities. As such he oversees about 38,000 persons, including 7,700 military, 660 Department of Defense civilians, 12,000 U.S. dependents, and 17,000 Philippine employees.

### Handling Combat Aircraft

The Clark headquarters of the Thirteenth Air Force is charged with command, control, administration, and logistical support for all operations in the West Pacific and, should circumstances require, for similar operations in the Indian Ocean. Clark is very well situated to mount an effective defense of the major sea lanes of communication in Southeast Asia and to inhibit any enemy combat operations in the area in time of overt conflict. Capable of supporting, servicing, and repairing more than 800 combat aircraft at a time, the base provides for the rapid deployment of U.S. armed might into the entire West Pacific, Southeast Asia, and the Indian Ocean. The Third Tactical Fighter Wing has combat-ready aircraft and flight crews that can be quickly activated by an array of major satellite intelligence, radio communications, and active defense alert systems operated by the 1961st Communications Group stationed at Clark.[8]

Should rapid response to developments in the Middle East be necessary, Clark would serve as a major departure point for fighter aircraft and interceptors. Launched from somewhere other than the Philippines, F-4 Phantoms would require more inflight refuelings to reach their destination. They would also require more over-flight clearances from other countries in the region; the Philippine facilities offer direct flight paths. Despite advances in aerial refueling techniques, in any conflict the availability of Clark would permit more air power to remain on station over the sea lanes of Southeast Asia than would be possible otherwise. Clark Air Base, bases in Kadena, Okinawa, Yokota Air Base in Japan, and Anderson Air Base in Guam together form a network that enables the United States to provide land-based air cover to the shipping lanes in East Asia.

### Logistical Support and Other Services

The base is responsible for airlift operations within the Pacific Command and can handle about 3,500 short tons of cargo daily. During the Vietnam War, Clark staged very large operations. Its major runway, 10,500 feet long, can accommodate the largest transport aircraft, including the C-5 Galaxy, which can carry a freight load of two M-1 battle tanks, or five M-113 armored personnel carriers, or about 300 fully armed troops, for a maximum payload of about 265,000 pounds. In a normal month, Clark handles an average of 1,500 transitting aircraft that carry supplies and personnel throughout the region.

In times of crisis, the base would be important for the direct launch of combat aircraft. But most critical to U.S. strategy would be its role as a major logistics hub through which all materiel would be redistributed to combat units on station or involved in forward movements. The U.S. facilities at Clark can store over 200,000 cubic feet of ammunition and 25 million gallons of fuel.[9] In addition, there are three million square feet of space (half a million under cover) in which some 100,000 items, ranging from portable control towers to transistors, are stored. A considerable amount of storage area is assigned to war readiness materiel, and the facilities could be rapidly expanded. To duplicate the storage space available at Clark would be very difficult.

In addition to its roles as a potential launch site in time of crisis and a logistical storehouse, Clark provides U.S. military forces in the West Pacific with a training, bombing, and gunnery range that greatly enhances their combat readiness. At the Crow Valley Range, in a corridor twelve miles long and seven miles wide, air crews use F-5E "aggressor aircraft" to simulate enemy intercept maneuvers and a network of target mock-ups defended by anti-aircraft and missile sites. This training could significantly reduce potential U.S. combat losses by seasoning flight crews to the demands of actual combat.

Clark Air Base also serves as the base of operations for the Air Force Regional Medical Center, which serves personnel of the West Pacific and Southeast Asia. With a 370-bed hospital capable of all types of care, the center was a major reception point for the wounded evacuated from Vietnam. It also has two completely mobile fifty-bed tactical hospitals.

## The Lesser Facilities

Among the smaller components of the network of U.S. military installations in the Philippines is the 454-acre Wallace Air Station at Poro Point. Wallace provides air control, radar coverage, and satellite intelligence relay for the Philippine Defense Zone. It maintains over-the-horizon surveillance along the sea lanes of communication through the South China Sea. It operates a live-fire range—one of only two maintained by the U.S. Air Force in the world—that extends over Philippine territorial waters into the South China Sea basin. The units stationed at Wallace also support tactical air training and deliver air-to-air services as necessary. They provide for the launch and control of target drones and remotely piloted vehicles used in the Pacific Air Force's weapon systems evaluation programs.

The John Hay Air Station, occupying 645 acres near the mountain city of Baguio north of Manila, is a rest and recreation facility maintained by the U.S. Air Force. It serves personnel from all branches of the U.S. and Philippine military services and plays an acknowledged role in maintaining troop morale in the East Asian theater. The camp also provides facilities for a Voice of America transmitter complex.

The Naval Communications Station at San Miguel consists of several stations that make up a communications network. The

San Miguel complex has about 550 U.S. military personnel attached to it and is essential to the effective operation of the Seventh Fleet, providing the fleet with radio, teletype, and microwave service both afloat and ashore. Its normal range of high-frequency radio transmission is about 1,500 nautical miles, and it also has very-low-frequency transmitting capabilities for contacting submerged nuclear-powered submarines.

The San Miguel communications network links military satellites over the Indian and Pacific oceans. It is one of the three "nodules"—the others are in Japan and South Korea—that operate a network of telecommunications lines from the West Pacific to military headquarters in Hawaii. All civil air traffic as well as the air defense requirements of the region are served by the communications facilities at San Miguel and the Wallace Air Station.

## THE U.S.-PHILIPPINE BASES AGREEMENT

The U.S. military presence in the Philippines is based on provisions of the 1946 Treaty of General Relations Between the United States and the Republic of the Philippines. That document, which granted independence to the Philippines, also reserved U.S. access to military bases in the archipelago. The treaty provisions were implemented by an executive agreement—the Military Bases Agreement—signed in 1947. This agreement was supplemented by a Military Assistance Agreement that entered into force in March 1947, a Mutual Defense Treaty signed in August 1951, and the multilateral Southeast Asia Collective Defense Treaty, September 1954.

As we have seen, almost from the start there were Philippine objections to the relationship. The Bases Agreement did not provide for any rental to be paid to the Philippines. Its term was long—the United States was to be allowed access for ninety-nine years. The U.S. base commander had complete jurisdiction over the conduct of both U.S. and Philippine personnel and over the use of the facilities. The United States had the right to use the bases in any manner it considered militarily advisable.

By the late 1950s so many objections were being raised that the United States entered into a Bases Agreement Amendment (the 1959 Bohlen-Serrano Agreement) requiring that use of the bases for combat operations other than those conducted in accordance with the U.S.-Philippine Mutual Defense Treaty or the Manila Pact be subject to prior consultation with Manila. The agreement was understood to prohibit offensive use of the bases without explicit agreement of the Philippine authorities.

While the use of the facilities for the war in Vietnam presumably was allowable under the Bohlen-Serrano Agreement, since the defense of Vietnam was undertaken under the provisions of the Manila Pact as part of the Southeast Asia collective defense arrangement, the United States chose to use the bases exclusively for logistical support rather than offensive operations so as not to abrade Philippine sensibilities.

### Changes in Jurisdiction

Throughout the years the Bases Agreement has been amended by an exchange of executive correspondence, most recently in June 1983. Perhaps the most important change came about in 1959, when the effective length of the 1947 agreement was reduced by more than half; the termination date is now 1991. Also, in 1966 revisions were made in the jurisdiction over criminal and civil matters in the base areas, as well as over the off-post activities of U.S. servicemen. The current arrangements conform to the status-of-forces formula governing North Atlantic Treaty Organization bases in Europe. Local authorities now have almost complete jurisdiction over all foreign (i.e., U.S.) personnel stationed on national territory.

The far-reaching amendments agreed upon in 1979 provide for a Philippine commander of each base site—with an American officer in command only of the actual U.S. facilities located on the larger base reservation. The U.S. facilities commanders, in effect, became tenants on the reservations.

The area actually under U.S. command was therefore substantially reduced. About 90 per cent of the acreage at Clark Air Force Base was returned to Philippine control. The U.S. commander now exercises control over no more than 10,410 acres of the 130,000 acres formerly under U.S. jurisdiction. The Crow Valley Weapons Range remains a special operating area, used for training by both the U.S. and the Philippine armed forces. The land under control of the U.S. facilities commander at Subic Bay was reduced from 62,000 to about 14,400 acres; 45 per cent of the land area and most of the waters of Subic Bay reverted to Philippine control. Similar reductions occurred at the minor base facilities elsewhere on Luzon.

In accordance with the new arrangements, the Philippine government assumed responsibility for the integrity of the bases, including perimeter security, although the U.S. commander remains responsible for internal security. The U.S. decision to surrender perimeter security followed from a number of unfortunate incidents in which U.S. security personnel were charged with arbitrary and excessive use of force against Filipinos attempting to enter the base grounds.

The United States is obliged by mutual agreement to consult the Philippine government if it considers any plans for installing long-range missile sites on Philippine soil. Similarly, Washington must inform Manila of any "major change" in weapon systems introduced into inventory on the Philippine bases.

Yet despite all these amendments, the United States continues to have relatively unfettered use of the bases.[10] The most recent amendments stipulate that the actual facilities within the base reservations remain under the effective control of the U.S. commanders, who "shall exercise command control over . . . military operations involving United States Forces." Moreover, use of the areas returned to Philippine control will not be allowed to interfere with U.S. military operations. In effect, the United States continues to "be assured unhampered military operations involving its forces in the Philippines."

### "Free of Rent"

The preamble to the 1947 Military Bases Agreement states that in the interests of mutual defense, the United States would be allowed to use designated bases "free of rent," and no amendments have altered this. From the start, the fiction that the use of the bases is rent free has been sustained: the United States "voluntarily" offers the Philippine government compensation in the form of military and economic aid.

The first such compensation package was arranged with the signing of the Bases Agreement in 1947. Since then, various presidents have entered into an agreement with Manila to make "best efforts" to obtain a military and economic aid package in return for use of the facilities. After a review of the Bases Agreement in 1979, President Jimmy Carter made such efforts to obtain $500 million in security assistance over a five-year period: $50 million in outright military grants, $250 million in foreign military sales credits, and $200 in economic support assistance. The economic aid was to be used to improve conditions in areas adjacent to the bases. After the most recent negotiations, in 1983, President Ronald Reagan undertook "best efforts" to provide $900 million in military and economic assistance over five years.

The prevailing procedure not only maintains the fiction that base use is rent free for the United States, and respects the U.S. constitutional provision that only the Congress can appropriate funds, but also allows the bases arrangement to remain an executive agreement, not subject to congressional ratification.

### Philippine Objections to the Agreement

Modifications have not defused all criticism. Critics object that the United States has agreed to far more lucrative arrangements with other countries that house bases for U.S. forces. In the late 1970s, for instance, the United States concluded a $1.2 billion five-year agreement with Spain, a $1 billion four-year agreement with Turkey, and a $700 million four-year agreement with Greece, for the use of facilities that are far less impressive than those in the Philippines. As late as 1978, moreover, even countries like Indonesia that have refused to tolerate foreign bases on their soil have received more in U.S. security assistance than the Philippines—despite the fact that the Philippine armed forces have had to contend with two major domestic insurrectionary movements.[11] Given the importance of the facilities in the archipelago, even Filipinos well disposed toward the United States have objected to the scant compensation.

Other Filipinos have objected to the bases arrangement on the grounds that "foreign forces" enjoy "extraterritorial" rights that violate Philippine sovereignty. They have maintained that the unhampered use of Philippine soil by U.S. troops constitutes a violation of national sovereignty and reduces the Republic of the Philippines to a client state of the United States. As we have seen, these arguments were heard with some frequency even before the Philippines became independent.

In addition, Filipinos have pointed out that the U.S. military reservations take about 210,000 acres of prime arable land out of production. Estimates are that the land so employed could produce 8.5 million cavans (1 cavan = 44 kilos) of husked rice. At the prevailing rate of rice, the land taken out of production might have contributed about $110 million to the national economy. Moreover, the occupation of that land denies property to the land-hungry peasants.[12]

Through the years, objections to the U.S. military presence in the Philippines have become increasingly acerbic. Critics have insisted that the bases serve U.S. interests only. Since the Republic of the Philippines is not under threat from any external power, the bases simply make the islands a target for any power involved in conflict with the United States. The Philippines, according to the argument, could be drawn into a conflict not of its own choosing and perhaps irrelevant to its national interests.[13] In a world with a surfeit of nuclear weapons capabilities, so exposed a position has nothing to recommend it.[14]

More recently, Philippine critics have maintained that the U.S. presence enables Washington to wield decisive influence over the conduct of Philippine affairs. Filipinos have cited U.S. intervention in peasant protests in the 1930s, 1940s, and 1950s as instances of American involvement in internal Philippine affairs. The U.S. bases were used in the suppression of peasant uprisings throughout the years of the commonwealth and in the immediate post-war period, when U.S. forces contributed to the defeat of the Huk uprisings in Luzon. Before the downfall of

Marcos, the opposition charged that Marcos remained in power against the will of the Philippine people only because the United States, concerned about the security of its bases, supported him. Had the concern for the bases not influenced U.S. political judgment, said the opposition, the people of the Philippines would have replaced Marcos with a more democratic ruler much sooner.[15]

### The Critics as Moderates

It is important to realize that these more recent objections to the U.S.-Philippine Military Bases Agreement do not emanate from Communist or "radical" sources. They are expressed by the leaders of the Philippine "moderate" opinion. In fact, in their most anti-American expression, these "moderate" objections constitute, as we shall see, a demand for the exclusion of U.S. economic and military influence from the archipelago.

In 1983, for example, former senators Jose Diokno and Lorenzo Tañada both wrote laudatory introductions to a volume by Roland C. Simbulan. They applauded Simbulan's charge that the U.S. bases contributed substantially to the exploitation and oppression of the Philippine people. Tañada identified Simbulan's exposition with the "dramatic awakening" of the Philippine people. That awakening made Filipinos aware of the "truth" that "the oppression and injustice perpetrated on [the Philippine] people" was undertaken in the service of "U.S. interests." The "true freedom, true independence, and true democracy" of the Philippines could emerge only with the expulsion of the U.S. military presence.[16]

Jose Diokno, who became a major functionary in the post-Marcos administration of Corazon Aquino (he died early in 1987), described the purposes of the U.S. bases as "not defense of the Philippines or of the United States, but to protect U.S. power in and consolidate U.S. dominance over Asia and the Middle East." Moreover, the U.S. military bases serve to "prevent the growth of industrialization . . . through the perpetuation of foreign control of [the national] economy." Finally, in Diokno's judgment, the U.S. military bases threaten to make the

Philippines a "sacrificial lamb on the altar . . . of U.S. ambitions to dominate the world."[17]

Once again, these are not "radical" sentiments emanating from neo-Marxists. As we shall see, such opinions figure in the political calculations of the most "moderate" political leaders in Manila.[18] They do not bode well for the future of the U.S. military facilities.

With the collapse of the Marcos administration, Corazon Aquino led a new political leadership to power in the Philippines. That leadership is by no means united concerning the future of the U.S. military presence in the islands. The entire relationship between the United States and the Philippines appears to be the object of a fundamental reassessment.

# 4

# *The Post-Marcos Succession*

THROUGHOUT MUCH of the 1970s, the Philippine economy maintained a creditable 6.4 per cent annual rate of real growth. Agricultural productivity increased at an annual rate of 5 per cent. Domestic capital formation proceeded apace, and the annual growth of real per capita income was sustained at about 3.6 per cent. As late as 1981, the World Bank could still applaud the Philippine economic performance for having hit the "principal targets" of its developmental program.[1]

By that time, however, the foreign debt had begun to impair that performance. Between 1960 and 1971, public debt grew at an annual rate of 13 per cent. Between 1972 and 1983 the rate escalated to 32.9 per cent, and in 1982–83 it was about 1,600 per cent.[2] By 1983 Philippine indebtedness was about $30 billion, and servicing that debt consumed about 40 per cent of the country's foreign exchange earnings. In that year the peso was devalued by about a third, from P 9.17 to the dollar to P 14 to the dollar. The consequence was an inflation rate of about 60 per cent.[3] The real growth rate collapsed to 1.4 per cent in 1983 and lapsed into negative growth in 1984.

Although a considerable portion of the Philippine economic woes at the start of the 1980s resulted from external influences over which Manila had little control, the islands' performance was measurably inferior to that of the other economies of the region. Between 1960 and 1980, the yearly real economic growth of the Philippines averaged 4.4 per cent, compared to 5.4 per cent for other non-Communist economies in Southeast Asia.

## *External Factors in the Economic Crisis*

The Philippine economy was severely damaged by the two large successive increases in the world price of oil. The country, dependent on imported oil for most of its energy, found its annual oil cost escalating from $197 million in 1973 to $651 million in 1974 and $2,078 million in 1982.

Moreover, over the same period the Philippines suffered a huge decline in the terms at which its exports were exchanged for imports on the world market. Between 1972 and 1982 these terms of trade collapsed from 100 to 55.6. This meant that in 1982 the country had to export roughly twice as much as it did in 1972 to purchase the same quantity of goods. Few developing economies that depend heavily on trade could absorb a 45 per cent deterioration in their terms of trade over a period of only ten years without experiencing major economic dislocations.[4]

Most of this decline was attributable to the rapid and steady erosion in the world price of primary commodities.[5] For example, the international price of sugar and coconut products, which make up a considerable portion of Philippine exports, had fallen to unprecedented low levels by the end of the 1970s. Thus, at a time when the cost of imported fuel was escalating, the earning capacity of the Philippine economy was being critically impaired.

The immediate consequence was a $1.1 billion balance-of-payments deficit in 1982, which caused a 46 per cent increase in the then current account imbalance of $3.3 billion.[6] That was followed by accelerated borrowing. External borrowing increased so rapidly that by 1983 about 85 per cent of all net capital inflow into the Philippines was in the form of capital loans.[7] This was at a time when only 15 per cent of capital inflow into Malaysia and only 5 per cent of such inflow into Singapore was made up of loans.

By the end of 1983, the annual payment on Manila's foreign debt, a payment that had been $370 million in the early 1970s, had ballooned to over $2 billion. And so at the same time that exports were covering less and less of the costs of imports, and domestic savings were proving incapable of meeting investment requirements, the cost of servicing the external debt grew much greater.

All these external factors were compounded by particular rigidities in the islands' economic system, some inherited by the

Marcos regime and others seemingly a function of the centraliza-
tion of power in the presidential palace. To add to the woes,
many of the loyalists whom Marcos had drawn around him gave
every evidence of incompetence, and in some cases corruption.
"Non-performing assets"—that is, debt-ridden and unprofitable
projects underwritten by the government—began to accumulate
throughout the system.

All this translated into a marked deterioration in the living
conditions of the majority of Filipinos. Unemployment and
underemployment increased as the agricultural sector was
forced to reduce production costs and as industries dismissed
workers because of the unavailability of short-term credit.
While no firm figures are available, estimates of unemployment
between 1982 and 1985 range as high as 25 to 30 per cent. The
population of entire sections of the country lapsed into marginal
subsistence, as coconut and sugar farmers found themselves
unable to provide for their families.

## The Growth of Opposition

The political consequences were predictable. There was an
appreciable decline in the support for President Marcos as
measured by probability samples drawn from the general population. In July 1982, in samples from metropolitan Manila, 75 per
cent expressed the conviction that the Kilusang Bagong Li-
punan, Marcos's New Society Party, was serving the people's
needs.[8] Since these surveys were confidential reports to the
executive office, there is reason to believe they were accurate
(assuming the data were collected responsibly). As late as July
1983, Marcos's performance was still rated positively by a
surprisingly large majority in samples drawn throughout the
archipelago.[9]

By 1984, however, his performance rating had fallen to 47 per
cent.[10] In September 1985 only 16.6 per cent of the respondents
voluntarily named Marcos as their preferred candidate in any
future presidential election, and only about 38 per cent said that
given a forced choice they would vote for him.[11] While a majority expected him to win in any future presidential election, and

little confidence was shown in any of the opposition leaders, it was clear that support for Marcos had eroded greatly between 1982 and the latter part of 1985. There was an almost perfect correlation between this decline in support and the collapse of the economy.

Both the economic collapse indicators and the erosion of support for Marcos were accelerated by the assassination of former senator Benigno Aquino on the tarmac of the Manila International Airport on August 21, 1983. This tragic murder of the most credible of the Marcos opponents upon his return to the Philippines from exile galvanized the opposition into action. Hundreds of thousands of Filipinos gave public expression to their dissatisfaction with Marcos, and the president and his inner circle were widely blamed for the Aquino murder. Given the perilous state of the economy, many anticipated the imminent collapse of the Marcos regime.[12]

Large segments of the business community had become disillusioned. With the imposition of martial law, Marcos had attempted to create a "Philippine Zaibatsu" of loyal entrepreneurs who could administer a developmental program for the archipelago. He provided these "cronies" with business advantages in exchange for their loyalty. Having the power to issue legislation at his discretion, Marcos regularly intervened in the islands' economic processes to favor those he had charged with developmental responsibility. There were literally hundreds of presidential decrees and letters of instruction designed to influence economic activities in agriculture, forestry, fishing, mining, quarrying, manufacturing, the provision of public utilities, construction, commerce, transportation, storage, communications, finance, insurance, and real estate. Even the nation's recreational and personal-service industries were directly influenced by interventions from the presidential palace.[13]

Whatever Marcos's motives might have been, these interventions were perceived by important members of the business community as nothing more than patronage. "Cronyism and corruption" became critical considerations among half the respondents in public opinion polls during the last years of the Marcos regime.

All this fed into the complaints of human rights violations that had been broadcast for years by the opposition. Government agencies were charged with violating the civil and political rights of thousands of citizens. Prominent figures in the Roman Catholic Church, a body that represented about 85 per cent of the population, became increasingly vocal in their objections to the regime.

### Rise of the Radical Left

As the economy veered toward collapse, the radical left opposition—the Communist Party of the Philippines and its armed contingent, the New People's Army (NPA)—began to grow rapidly. In 1980, when the economy was expanding at a reasonable pace, the estimated combat strength of the insurrectionary NPA was 2,000, and the group was considered little more than "troublesome."[14] The following year, as the economy began to lapse deeper into recession, the insurrectionary forces were reportedly growing "slowly but steadily."[15] By 1985, with the economy locked into negative growth, government intelligence estimates put the number of Communist insurrectionists at between 10,000 and 12,000 regulars—two-thirds of whom were armed.[16] A U.S. survey reported 16,500 insurgents in November 1985 and said Communist organizations had been established in a third of the nation's 41,400 barangays (the lowest unit of government administration).[17] By the end of 1985 about as many irregular combatants as there were regulars had enlisted in the NPA, and the total number active in the armed insurgency was around 30,000. Since about ten persons clustered around each of the NPA combatants, the insurrectionary forces had an active population support base of 300,000 persons.[18]

The government's counterinsurgency forces included about 70,000 combatants in the regular army and the marines. They were supported by about 43,500 members of the Philippine constabulary and about 65,000 to 70,000 irregulars organized in the Civilian Home Defense Forces (CHDF)—home guard units with very little training and the most rudimentary arms. These figures do not justify much confidence in the future ability of government forces to suppress the NPA in the field. Normally, counterinsurgency forces should outnumber insurgents ten to one if an anti-guerrilla campaign is to be successful. The forces available to the Philippine military fall considerably short of that—particularly if one discounts CHDF units, which are of marginal military utility. To these numerical disabilities must be added the fact that the regular Armed Forces of the Philippines (AFP)—to say nothing of the irregular units—suffer from a severe deficiency of supplies of all kinds.[19]

### Fellow-Traveling on the Left

The Communist Party of the Philippines maintains a "united front" organization—the NDF, National Democratic Front—that recruits members who, though not prepared to join the party, in essence agree with its political goals. A number of left-wing organizations have collected around the NDF in the past and have continued to influence events.

Groups like the Christian Liberation Army, the April Sixth Movement, and Bayan—an umbrella organization led by a collection of left-of-center political figures (the late Jose Diokno was one)—are the "fellow travelers" of the radical left. These groups generally address a trio of themes: (1) the exploitative character of U.S.-Philippine relations; (2) the necessity to reorient the Philippine economy so that it is "self-sufficient," and to address the nation's needs rather than those of the international export market; and (3) the threats posed by the U.S. military presence in the islands, and the recommendation that all "foreign bases" in the Philippines be evacuated.

Even those who advertise themselves as "non-Marxists" exploit the same themes. Renato Constantino, for example, the dean of Philippine "nationalism," has insisted that the republic remains subjected to "neocolonial" oppression; that the United States systematically labors to "perpetuate poverty and underdevelopment" in the islands; that the relation between the "imperialist" United States and the Philippines is fundamentally adversarial; that the "nationalist position" on the U.S. bases has always been that "they . . . should be dismantled"; and, finally, that the republic should avail itself of the "assistance of socialist . . . countries" in order to break away from the oppressive embrace of the United States.[20]

Convinced that there is an inexhaustible reservoir of good will toward the United States among Filipinos, Americans tend to deny the pervasiveness of these kinds of convictions. To disabuse oneself of such a tendency, one need only consider the views of such respected figures as Elmer Abueg, economics chairman at "conservative" De La Salle University's Graduate School of Business and Economics; Perfecto V. Fernandez, professor of constitutional law at the University of the Philippines College of Law; and Vivencio R. Jose, director of the Philippine Studies Program at the University of the Philippines.

In Abueg's judgment, whenever a country "comes into the orbit of Western capitalist expansion," it falls under the "impact of imperialist subjugation." The solution he advocates is "to say 'no' to international forces and pressures." Fernandez and Jose, similarly, speak of "the colonial system of exploitation" under which the "captive economy" of the Philippines languishes. They use the term "U.S. imperialism" as though it represented a clear reality in the modern world. Jose has recommended total debt repudiation as a solution to the debt problem of the Philippines. It would represent "a just repayment for what historically has been taken away—through plunder and exploitation," he said. "Repudiation is not only our right as Filipinos, it is also in this context a blow against neocolonialism."[21]

Such opinions have become characteristic of a surprisingly large number of scholars and researchers in the mainstream institutions of the Philippines. Academics regale themselves with accounts of "capitalist exploitation"—and "moderate" political leaders such as the late Jose Diokno write concurring introductions to their works.[22] As a consequence, there is substantial support in the Philippines, particularly in urban areas, for a view of the United States as an "oppressor" whose activities are all part of the "machinery of oppression."

These views are not restricted to academia. Letizia R. Constantino (the wife of the aforementioned Renato Constantino) received a grant from the Catholic Church in the Philippines—through the offices of the Association of Major Religious Superiors—to supplement the education of Filipinos with her views on a variety of subjects, including how one might distinguish a true Philippine political leader from a lackey of imperialism. The true Filipinos, in her judgment, would "denounce" foreign economic domination, condemn U.S. support for authoritarianism, and demand the dismantling of the American military bases on Philippine soil.[23]

These opinions and the persons who entertain them are generally characterized as "moderate" and "democratic" by commentators in the United States. Many of them might indeed qualify as "democratic" in some meaningful sense, but it is hard to recognize their conception of U.S.-Philippine relations as "moderate." In Leif Rosenberger's judgment, by 1984 "less and less . . . distinguished the moderate from the radical anti-Marcos opposition in terms of American economic and security interests."[24] Organizations such as the Movement for Philippine Sovereignty and Democracy, the Anti-U.S. Bases Coalition, and the Coalition for the Restoration of Democracy take positions that are hardly distinguishable from those of their "radical" counterparts in the illegal and legal left alliance in Bayan, the Partido Ng Bayan, and the National Democratic Front—all intimately connected with the outlawed Communist Party of the Philippines.

These groups convey the conviction that the United States was the architect of all the disabilities of the Philippines. Marcos at his worst was only an instrument. All this has ensured that enmity toward the United States would survive long after the Marcos regime had become history.[25]

### The Human Rights Issue

Among the themes that remained constant among the opposition through the years of struggle against Marcos was the derogation of human rights attributed to the "dictatorship." More often than not, the issue was portrayed as inextricably bound up with the "imperialist interests" of the United States.

The United States was understood to have created the "Marcos dictatorship" or at least to have perpetuated it through direct and indirect support. As early as 1975, Lorenzo Tañada and Jose Diokno arranged to have published, under the imprimatur of the Civil Liberties Union of the Philippines, an account of human rights violations that attributed the very existence of the Marcos government to Washington's efforts "to protect the privileged position of foreign and domestic capital and the interests of the U.S. government." Those interests included the protection of "U.S. investments and U.S. [military] bases."[26]

Such arguments directly or by implication made the United States responsible for human rights violations in the Philippines. More than that, the entire issue of human rights came to involve the Armed Forces of the Philippines in a manner that could have grave implications for the future of the republic. The list of abuses attributed to the Philippine military by various social-action groups, church-affiliated associations, and lawyers' professional committees includes nearly every infamy imaginable. If every rumor were true, hardly a single soldier could escape condemnation.

In a book published by McGraw-Hill in 1984, Fred Poole and Max Vanzi collected all the rumors and bits of hearsay circulated in the Philippines that bear on these charges. The composite picture of the military man that emerges from their account is that of a sexual sadist, a thief, a liar, a defamer of nuns and clergymen, a murderer of women and children, and an unreflecting tool of his criminal superiors.[27] The leaders of the military in general—and specifically Juan Ponce Enrile, who became Corazon Aquino's minister of defense—are said to have exploited rank and position for personal enrichment. Furthermore, Enrile is said to have suppressed evidence of human rights violations while he systematically abused the privileges of his office.[28] General Fidel Ramos, commander of the Philippine Constabulary and an "unshakable Marcos loyalist," is similarly seen as a consummate liar who systematically concealed the human rights violations of his subordinates. Members of the constabulary were among the most grievous offenders, according to the opposition "watch groups."

In effect, by the last years of the Marcos incumbency the entire Philippine military had been discredited by the opposition movement. It was accepted as fact that the military had murdered an indeterminate number of people—massacring thousands at a time. Rape, torture, and robbery by the military were considered commonplace, ordered by the government or condoned by military leaders through their collective silence.

The entire human rights issue was employed effectively by the anti-Marcos opposition, and it had important effects in the United States, particularly in Congress, where the Philippine government was regularly taken to task for derogations. In fact, the anti-Marcos lobbyists (who made up one of the most effective lobbies in Washington[29]) damaged the credibility of the Marcos government substantially by focusing on human rights on every occasion. Constant repetition of the catalog of abuses attributed to the Marcos administration rapidly eroded the support the regime had among legislators and journalists in the United States.

The anti-Marcos human rights groups implicated the United States in the putative horror—thereby jeopardizing U.S. economic and security interests in any post-Marcos political environment. More seriously, they thoroughly discredited the armed forces of the nation. Even without Ferdinand Marcos, the Philippine military would continue to be perceived as a criminal organization.

## 1986: Advent of "People's Power"

As Ferdinand Marcos progressively lost his grip on political power, he took a desperate gamble. To certify his claim that he had a mandate to rule, he called for "snap elections" before a presidential election was constitutionally required.

Several factors apparently entered into that decision. One was that his health was fragile, and he might not be up to the rigors of an election campaign in 1987, when the next presidential election was scheduled. Moreover, should the economy deteriorate further, his support would surely erode as well. Also, the fact that his opponents were poorly organized recommended an early contest before they could effectively establish themselves throughout the country's seventy-three provinces. Finally, polls conducted by an independent sampling agency showed that at least 52 per cent of respondents expected Marcos to win in any future election.[30]

The elections of February 7, 1986, are now history, but we still do not have a probative tally of the results. Corazon Aquino, supported by "people's power," simply declared herself president of an "interim government" that would rule the Philippines until democracy could be restored. Most Americans who cared were too gratified by the turn of events to pursue the matter any further, and most Filipinos were immensely relieved that the post-Marcos era had been ushered in without bloodshed. But it is very unlikely that "people's power" would have prevailed in Manila if the two principal leaders of the Philippine military had not defected, at a most auspicious time, to the Aquino camp. When the minister of national defense, Juan Ponce Enrile, and the chief of staff of the Philippine military establishment, General Fidel Ramos, threw their support to Aquino's initiative, a potentially explosive situation was transformed into a peaceful, if irregular, transfer of power.

It is clear that Aquino, by and large, had the support of the Manila business community. She also had broad-based support among the urbanites of Manila, students, and the highly visible representatives of the clergy. Without the defection of the military, however, the situation would have been very difficult.

What this means is that the peaceful transfer of power was made possible by the incorporation into the new government of the two men most often identified as the "architects of Marcos's martial law regime." In photos that appeared immediately after Marcos took flight from Manila, Juan Ponce Enrile is seen sitting at President Aquino's side. The symbolism was very clear. The difficulties that attend that kind of accommodation, however, are obvious.

Corazon Aquino, while she was engaged in opposition to the Marcos government, frequently asserted that the military was responsible for the murder of her husband. The most aggressive supporters of her candidacy against Marcos were convinced that the Philippine military was little more than a gang of criminal sadists. The accommodation could only generate multiple tensions among the new president's followers. Those who had suffered for the integrity of "people's power" against the "corrupt dictatorship" found themselves in league with those who had long been identified as the mailed fist of the Marcos regime.

While the defection was causing difficulties among the now victorious anti-Marcos opposition, the presence in the government of Juan Ponce Enrile and Fidel Ramos brought considerable relief to American officials. For years both Enrile and Ramos had been known to be well disposed toward the United States. Members of the United States Mission in Manila were never coy about advocating Ramos's promotion to military chief of staff. Unlike Fabian Ver, Marcos's own choice for the position, Ramos had constructive and responsible relations with his American counterparts. "Johnny" Enrile, too, had had warm relations with Americans throughout his tenure in public office.

In effect, the defection of the leaders of the Philippine military from the ranks of Marcos loyalists transformed a situation that might have been a setback for U.S. policy into one in which that policy appeared to triumph. The presence of Enrile and Ramos gave a firm pro-American character to the Aquino government.

### A Tempering of "Anti-Foreign" Views

Of course, by the time of the elections, both Corazon Aquino and Salvador Laurel (who was to become Aquino's vice president) had already begun to back away from some positions they had previously assumed. While jockeying for advantage among the anti-Marcos opposition, both had committed themselves to a "review" of the economic relations between the Philippines and "foreign powers," and to an evacuation of the Americans from the military bases. Lorenzo Tañada, whose views on the "U.S. connection" were very well known, had been Corazon Aquino's close advisor when she convened the opposition to put together the Unity Principles that certified her opposition to the U.S. military bases.

When the prospects of her accession to the presidency improved, Aquino began to reformulate her position so as not to alarm the Americans unduly. The bases would be allowed to remain until the termination of the Military Bases Agreement in 1991. After that "all options" would be "open." For his part, Salvador Laurel abandoned his insistence on an "anti-foreign alternative economic policy," as well as his commitment to the abrogation of the bases agreement. By the time "people's power" brought the Aquino administration to office, Laurel was being characterized as "a friend of America."

While the qualifiers introduced by Aquino and Laurel into their pre-election commitments were heartening to American officials, only the defection of the military leaders from the Marcos camp into leadership roles among the revolutionaries allowed those officials to observe the collapse of the Marcos administration without qualms.

### Strange Bedfellows

But for all those who had anticipated that "people's power" would free the Philippines from the "trammels of U.S. imperialism," the Aquino accommodation with Enrile and Ramos could only constitute betrayal of the revolution. It was obvious that the swearing in of the new president after the flight of Ferdinand Marcos would be little more than the opening phase of very complicated political maneuvering. The difficulty is perhaps best illustrated by the case of Jose Diokno. Diokno had argued for years that the salvation of the Philippines required not only dismantling the Marcos political apparatus but (1) terminating the "neocolonial" economic relationship with the United States and (2) removing the U.S. military presence from the archipelago. He had also spent a great deal of energy identifying and cataloging military infractions of human rights in the islands.

Diokno served as head of the Human Rights Commission in the new Aquino administration until his death early in 1987. Like others, he found himself aligned with military leaders whom he had castigated for years. And like others, he faced a dilemma. If he pursued those members of the military he had long maligned, he might destabilize the delicately balanced political situation.

Therefore, while he insisted he would pursue all "malefactors" in the military, during his tenure he did not bring actionable charges against anyone.

Problems of this sort continue to afflict the administration in Manila. As noted earlier, President Aquino's cabinet is filled with political leaders who signed principled commitments to "review all economic arrangements and financial agreements with foreign governments," an obvious allusion to the arrangements the Marcos administration had made with the United States. These leaders had also called for the removal of foreign military bases and the legalization of the Communist Party of the Philippines.[31] But it is extremely unlikely that President Aquino could implement any of those changes without producing grave political consequences for her government.

Many had foreseen this situation and had warned Aquino's followers that as the prospects of a successful transfer of power improved, the most radical demands of the opposition would be tempered. Letizia Constantino told her followers:

> When the prospect of gaining political power seemed dark and distant, a number of opposition leaders projected in their party programs and individual statements more or less strong adherence to a nationalist, anti-imperialist perspective. We heard denunciations of foreign economic domination, demands for the dismantling of the bases. . . . Now that they can see the light at the end of the tunnel, now that political power is a likelihood rather than a remote possibility, some appear to be moderating their views or simply dropping controversial subjects from their political discourse.[32]

At the end of Corazon Aquino's first year in office, those who had labored and sacrificed for the advent of "people's power" were still waiting for her to give substance to their revolution.

## The Present Situation

With the abolition of the constitution of 1973 that had provided the legal basis of the Marcos regime, and the dismissal of all the provincial and local leaders who were loyal to the former president, Corazon Aquino found herself the single most powerful person in Philippine political history. Empowered with the authority to issue decree legislation, she appointed a special commission to write a new constitution. With power she provided herself as leader of the interim government she proclaimed, Corazon Aquino had chosen to do something Ferdinand Marcos had been unable to do: rewrite the constitution through a committee chosen by the executive office itself. The new constitution received the resounding support of the people in February 1987, and the vote served as a major new source of legitimacy for the Aquino presidency.

But for all its seeming power, the Aquino government is characterized by deep and perhaps fatal divisions. Both Aquino and Vice President Salvador Laurel have at various times espoused widely varying conceptions of the Philippine future. Moreover, in the present cabinet are persons who signed pledges to "reorient" the Philippine economy away from its "neocolonialist" traditions. There are those who have announced their irreversible opposition to the presence of "foreign troops" on Philippine soil. Lorenzo Tañada remains an advisor to the president—as well as chairman of the Nationalist Alliance for Justice, Freedom, and Democracy, which calls for a "dismantling of the U.S. military bases" and advocates nationalization of all those "basic industries" owned by "foreign capital." Jaime Ongpin, who officially affirmed his commitment to the removal of "foreign troops" from national territory, remains finance minister in the Aquino cabinet. And Ramon Mitra, the minister of agriculture, has announced such a commitment as well.

At the same time, the military is represented by Rafael Ileto, the successor to Juan Ponce Enrile—a man who has reaffirmed the commitments of the former minister of defense. General Fidel Ramos, in command of the armed forces, remains as steadfastly oriented toward the United States as he was at the time of the transition from the Marcos to the Aquino administration.

For her part, Corazon Aquino has had to accommodate to political reality. The loyalty of the military is a necessary support for the new government. At the same time, Aquino cannot alienate those political leaders who have grave reservations about the military. These leaders provided her with the popular support she needed for overt legitimacy before her constitution received majority support in February 1987. It was partially to accommodate them that she dismissed Enrile as her minister of defense in late November 1986.

### Business and Religious Views

The business community has always been fundamentally reformist in character and has sought little more than the kind of political stability that will allow businessmen to pursue their interests without undue obstruction, compete effectively in the major international markets, attract the necessary foreign investment, gain access to short-term credit, and operate in a domestic environment free from excessive government interference. The business community is disposed to support a government of reform, foster an export-oriented strategy of growth, and meet Philippine international obligations through a rational policy of steady economic modernization. The containment and ultimate suppression of the domestic insurgency would be a function of steadfast policy and a combination of armed force and socioeconomic initiatives.

The Roman Catholic Church in the Philippines, for its part, remains essentially conservative in its intentions. Having been embarrassed by recent evidence of extensive Communist inroads into its institutional structure, the church is attempting to control its more "progressive" elements.[33] The evidence that church funds had been used in the active service of the Communist Party was enough to chasten church leaders. The church's interests, like those of the business community, are compatible with a stable and productive relationship with the United States. And it appears reasonably certain that the church leadership is prepared to support a government of reform.

Such a government would require considerable austerity through the rest of the 1980s, and would have to exercise the control necessary to ensure containment of the Communist insurgency. That would be followed by slowly accelerating economic expansion in the early 1990s until the republic commenced a period of fairly rapid self-sustained growth.

Compatible with that scenario is the fact that the new administration asked associates of Bernardo Villegas for assistance in planning economic development. Villegas is head of the Center for Research and Communication, a free-trade-oriented economic think tank in Manila that is very well regarded in the United States. A set of proposals for national rehabilitation prepared by the center in 1985 outlined a pattern of economic growth based on some of the principal strategies of Asia's "little tigers," the market-governed economies of the Republic of Korea and the Republic of China on Taiwan.[34]

## The Complicating Factors

There is a potential for responsible political and economic development under the new administration in Manila. But some less constructive alternatives are possible as well.

As we have seen, the Philippine military is very vulnerable, in view of the long and systematic list of human rights abuses attributed to it throughout the almost twenty years of Marcos's rule. Given the accounts bruited by the anti-Marcos opposition throughout the period, at least half the rank and file of the military and all of its leadership could be considered criminally culpable. When the late Jose Diokno became head of the Human Rights Commission, he was in a position to initiate proceedings that could jeopardize the delicate political balance.

Diokno was also named an official government representative in the government's talks with the Communist insurgents. One of the conditions that the leaders of the insurgency have identified as central is the "kicking out of criminal and fascist elements from the army"—a demand understood to include "Enrile, and Ramos, and their stooges in the military who faithfully served the Marcos regime."[35] Enrile has already been dismissed. It was the responsibility of Diokno, who had himself made similar statements in the past, to deal with the representatives of the Communist insurgents. Many others who remain in positions of authority are similarly capable of creating problems not only for the Aquino administration and the Philippine republic but for the United States as well.

## The Immediate Challenges

The Aquino administration is likely to face a number of challenges in the immediate future that will test its capacity to survive. Within the government a number of persons either are dissatisfied with their positions in the new distribution of power or have been disillusioned by the compromises into which President Aquino has entered. Similar problems afflict almost any new government. The difference here is that in the near term and for the foreseeable future, the administration will not be able to mitigate the most damaging disabilities. It will not have the resources or the necessary conditions to solve the nation's economic, political, or insurrectionary problems.

The most generous estimates concerning the Philippine economy anticipate very low rates of real growth until the 1990s—and the probability of realizing even those rates is not high. In an economy in negative or negligible growth, unemployment will escalate and wages will decline, with increased labor militancy the predictable consequence. Over the next three years about 2.1 million new workers will enter the job market. Increasing unemployment will foster a new militancy among urban workers. Already a new labor organization—the four-year-old, 600,000-member, left-oriented Kulusang Mayo Uno (KMU, or May First Movement)—has committed itself to fundamental economic and political change.

The austerity required by international financial institutions will only increase the size and complexity of the problems and further reduce the options available to the Aquino government. In both urban and rural areas, distress will probably grow in the near term and persist for the foreseeable future.

What this means is that the guerrillas of the New People's Army can count on further recruitment successes, survival advantages, and urban support. This strengthening will reduce the possibility of a negotiated settlement between them and the Aquino government. As the NPA forces expand their numbers and their revenue—collected as "revolutionary taxes" from agribusiness throughout the islands—their indisposition to lay down their arms will necessarily increase. With added funding the NPA will attract still more active combatants and will be able to provide them with firepower in the field.

The military will find its response increasingly impaired by imposed austerity, and its morale will decline still further. Under Marcos, the military budget made up about 1.1 per cent of the nation's gross national product—the lowest allocation in Southeast Asia. With the austerity government that Aquino will be compelled to impose, the military can expect even less. The United States, for its part, has indicated that because of its own budget problems it cannot rescue the Philippines. Given the present level of military assistance forthcoming from Washington, the Armed Forces of the Philippines probably will not significantly improve its field capabilities in the short term.

### A Possible Communist-"Moderate" Alliance

The armed Communist insurgents in the countryside will accede to a permanent ceasefire only if it permits them the prospect of greater success. That might be effected by an alliance between the left-wing "moderates" and the increasingly effective urban Communist political organizations. Such an alliance would provide a broad popular base for a return to the principled "anti-imperialist" policies advocated by almost the entire anti-Marcos opposition before the "February revolution."

Under such circumstances the Philippine military would find its real and potential interests seriously compromised. Not only its Communist enemy but also representatives of the left, which has long identified the Philippine military with massive human rights derogations, would be playing a role in the government. Such developments would jeopardize the integrity of the military as an institution and also the lives and fortunes of armed forces personnel.

Aquino's attempt to forestall such a scenario has included the November 1986 firing of some of her controversial and left-oriented ministers. Nonetheless, some who have been identified as anti-American remain in the government, and it is unclear whether the effort to "balance" the administration after the dismissal of Juan Ponce Enrile will be successful in the long term. The suspicion remains that the Aquino administration is far too accommodating of the left and more than a little unrealistic about the prospects of peace with the armed Communist insurgency.

Should the government become a captive of the populist left, its "anti-imperialism" could very easily serve the interests of the Soviet Union. For instance, any effort to default on the Philippine foreign debt as part of an anti-imperialist policy would reduce Manila to abject dependency on the support of Eastern-bloc nations. Moscow would no doubt be prepared to underwrite the Philippine economy in much the same way that it subsidizes the economies of Cuba and Vietnam. The benefits Moscow would receive as compensation are obvious.

## The Future of the U.S. Military Presence

Under any variant of such a scenario, the U.S. military facilities in the Philippines would be exposed to serious threats. For several years, it has been common knowledge that NPA combatants have penetrated the perimeter of both Clark Field and the Subic Bay naval base.[36] To date, leaders of the Communist forces have been very circumspect about engaging U.S. interests directly. Nonetheless, under an easily conceivable set of circumstances, the NPA might want to bring pressure on the Aquino government by setting off a confrontation within the precincts of the military bases. The government would then be faced with three equally unattractive alternatives: (1) permitting the U.S. government to reestablish its own perimeter defenses (at the real or apparent expense of Philippine "sovereignty"); (2) using Philippine troops to defend the U.S. facilities, thereby risking the opprobrium of employing Filipinos to kill Filipinos in defense of Americans; or (3) requiring U.S. evacuation of the facilities.

Even without NPA initiatives, renegotiations on the Military Bases Agreement will have to be undertaken in 1988–89. At that point, the Aquino government will probably insist on high compensation for the use of the bases without necessarily making any commitment to renew the agreement in 1991. How the negotiations progress in 1988 will of course be significantly influenced by political conditions in the archipelago at that time.

At present, the leaders of the Philippines seem inclined to put the question of U.S. access to military facilities in the islands to a national referendum. Whether this course of action will ultimately be chosen, and what the outcome might be, cannot now be foreseen. Between May and September 1985, at least three polls inquired into Philippine attitudes toward the U.S. military presence. All showed a plurality favoring retention of U.S. access ranging from 36.2 per cent to 43 per cent. Those opposed ranged from 23 per cent to 34.9 per cent. In each poll about a third of the respondents were undecided.[37] In effect, there is not a broad and deep reservoir of support for continuing to accept the U.S. military presence in the islands.

## The Pro-Western Constituency

On the other hand, a relatively small but firm constituency has collected around the military bases. After the Philippine government itself, the U.S. Department of Defense is the single largest employer in the islands, paying out about $330 million annually to about 35,000 Filipinos. These persons have a vested interest in the U.S.-Philippine bases arrangement. In addition, the United States is committed to providing $900 million in compensation for base use between 1984 and 1989. Finally, U.S. servicemen spend about $60 million annually onshore in the vicinity of the bases and have attracted corresponding support.

On the whole, the United States contributes about 3 to 5 per cent of the gross domestic product of the Philippines as a consequence of the Military Bases Agreement.[38] Individuals and groups that directly benefit from these infusions form a substantial body of support. From what Enrile has said to date, it seems clear that he would be the spokesman for this group.

A coalition of the military, active business elements, and church representatives could provide the core of an essentially pro-Western political system in the Philippines. That system would provide the foundation for a pro-American, export-oriented growth economy, and that economy would support the security agreements that uphold the prevailing stability in Southeast Asia.

The principal source of threat to that stability in the Philippines is the complex economic problems that have settled down over the archipelago. The anti-American elements will exploit those problems to their own advantage. Moscow is adept at gaining access to troubled political environments, and it has every reason to be interested in developments in the Philippines.[39] At the moment, the Soviet Union has entree into many of the labor and political organizations that have proliferated throughout the islands. Representatives of the left wing in domestic politics, nationalists, and enthusiasts of "liberation theology" in the religious community would all be amenable to overtures from Moscow's "anti-imperialist progressives."

Add to this mix those in the Aquino government who are discontent with the maintenance of economic and security ties with "imperialism," and there is the potential for an alternative politics that would reverse the pro-U.S. policies of the past. Such a reversal not only would impair U.S. economic and security interests but also might destabilize the entire southeast Asian quadrant of the Pacific.

# 5

# *Alternative Basing Arrangements*

THE BERTHING, PARKING, STORAGE, servicing, repair, housing, training, and logistical capabilities provided by the Philippine bases are essential if U.S. forces are to carry out their mission of supporting operations in Southeast Asia, contributing to any undertakings in Northeast Asia, and, as they have been called upon to do, supporting operations in the Indian Ocean and Persian Gulf regions.[1] The political instability and the potential for radical change in the Philippines have made it necessary for U.S. security analysts to contemplate the possibility of being forced to relocate these facilities.

Three options have evolved. They are: (1) transferring the facilities to other existing U.S. Pacific bases; (2) building new facilities in the Marianas (the islands of Tinian and Saipan) and Micronesia (Palau Island); and (3) negotiating with one or more new host nations for permission to establish U.S. base facilities on their territories.[2]

As we have seen, the primary objective of U.S. naval and air forces in Southeast Asia is to act as a deterrent to misadventure by any military actor in the region. Those forces must be prepared to suppress enemy air and naval units that threaten the routes threading through the South China Sea and the chokepoints serving as entry and exit from the region. The potential control exercised by U.S. forces over Soviet supply lines to their Vietnamese bases and their military installations in Northeast Asia serves as both a deterrent to conflict and a critical warfighting capability. The Philippine bases facilitate such operations because they afford easy access to the sea and air routes of the South China Sea, those to the east of the Philippines, and those from the Indonesian Straits to Northeast Asia. Moreover, the Philippine bases are within effective tactical strike range of the Soviet bases in Vietnam.

The U.S. bases in the Philippines allow for ready defense of the sea lanes of communication in the South China Sea region and provide some assurance that in crisis circumstances the energy needs of the Northeast Asian theater would be met. That assurance is of fundamental importance to Japan and the Republic of Korea.

Finally, military operations in the Persian Gulf region depend heavily on U.S. access to the Indian Ocean via sea and air routes in Southeast Asia. Keeping the Soviet Union from controlling those passageways is essential to the enterprise. As we have seen, Subic Bay and Clark Air Base constitute a major logistical hub for naval and air projection into the Indian Ocean and Persian Gulf regions.

Alternatives to the present basing arrangements must be assessed first against these responsibilities and the capabilities they require, and that is how we shall proceed in this chapter. Costs and political feasibility are secondary considerations.[3]

## MOVING THE FACILITIES TO EXISTING BASES

One obvious option is to transfer the facilities to U.S. bases already operational in the Pacific west of Hawaii. The principal advantage of this option is its ready availability. There are U.S. military bases in Japan, Okinawa, and Guam to which the support structures and services now in the Philippines could be added.

### The Base at Yokosuka

The fleet maintenance functions carried out at Subic Bay could be relocated at Yokosuka, Japan. Indeed, this work was previously done there, before Subic was expanded during the Vietnam conflict. The repair facilities at Yokosuka compare favorably with those at Subic and indeed surpass Subic's in one way: they can bring a carrier into dry dock. The largest attack and multi-purpose aircraft carriers can be berthed and serviced there.

In other ways, however, the Subic Bay facilities are superior. Aircraft cannot be removed from carriers for station repair at Yokosuka. While Yokosuka has a larger storage capacity for fuel and lubricants, Subic currently distributes more fuel, and its storage is more secure. Subic Bay operates its overhauling, repair, alterations, and conversion service twenty-four hours a day, year round, and far more is invested in capital equipment there than at Yokosuka. More services can be provided at Subic not only because of the larger investment in capital equipment but also because labor costs there are significantly lower. In 1978 a twelve-hour man day cost $29 in the Philippines, compared to $179 in Japan.[4]

## The Base on Guam

Guam offers an excellent harbor with 80 per cent of the berthing capacity of Pearl Harbor. Since Guam is U.S. territory, the tenure of bases there is secure. The Guam Naval Supply Depot is large and can probably meet support requirements for vessels of the Seventh Fleet. Agana Naval Air Station can host an entire carrier air group. A newly constructed naval ammunition pier at Apra Harbor can handle fleet ordnance requirements. There are plans to expand fuel storage reservoirs.

Operational shortcomings at Guam include a narrow harbor entrance and relatively shallow harbor depth. The harbor cannot accommodate the larger cruisers of the U.S. Navy or aircraft carriers, which require a greater turning radius and a harbor depth of about thirty-seven feet.

Guam, moreover, is in the typhoon belt, and weather problems can interfere with naval and air operations. Since the island's population is only about 100,000, Guam could not assume all the functions of Subic Bay, which employs about 25,000 local residents.[5]

To expect the U.S. bases in Japan and Guam, individually or in combination, to absorb the operational responsibilities of the Thirteenth Air Force is unrealistic in the short and medium term. The U.S. Air Force currently bases strategic bombers and their refueling tankers on Guam and F-15 Eagle fighters in Okinawa and Japan. The Marine Corps bases F-4 Phantoms, F-18 Hornets, A-6 Intruders, and A-4 Skyhawks in Japan. The U.S. Navy stations P-3 Orions on Guam and the Japanese home islands. Relocating the tactical fighter wing and the tactical airlift wing from Clark Air Base to Japan or Guam would quickly overload the facilities at either site. Considerable base expansion would be necessary. Any expansion in the crowded Japanese islands would require the acquisition of prime land—something that might very well be prohibitive both in cost and in Japanese political repercussions. An increased American military presence in Japan with expanded base facilities could trigger significant domestic resistance.

Agana Naval Air Station on Guam might be able to accommodate the airlift functions of Clark, but it could not take over both the tactical airlift wing and the tactical fighters. It is conceivable that with some expansion, all the existing U.S. facilities west of Hawaii—the bases in Japan, Okinawa, and Guam—could together absorb all the Philippine functions.

### The Geographical Drawback

Even if that could be accomplished, however, there is a very basic problem of geography. Japan, Okinawa, and Guam are all far away from Southeast Asia. Relocation to any of these sites would therefore compromise at least two of the military functions fulfilled by Philippine bases.

From Japan or Guam, the increased travel time necessary to reach stations in Southeast Asia or the Indian Ocean and Persian Gulf regions would make naval and air forces less credible deterrents in peace and less effective combatants in conflict. Forces located in Japan or Guam would be 1,500 to 2,000 miles away from their operational stations. Their time on station in Southeast Asia and the Indian Ocean would therefore be reduced by about 20 per cent.[6] The theater military command would probably have to do one of two things: reduce the U.S. military presence in those areas, or build additional carrier battle groups and support forces to discharge the time-sensitive tasks presently assigned to units in the Philippines.

In time of conflict, at least two additional carrier battle groups would be needed. The estimated cost of one such group, fully equipped, is $17 billion. The alternative to that additional defense outlay would be to suffer the loss of available air cover, reduce the number of ship days in which naval forces remain on station in Southeast Asia and the Indian Ocean, and tolerate the resultant erosion in the credibility of the U.S. deterrent.

To sum up: relocation of the Philippine bases to Japan and Guam would initially involve a considerable loss in operational effectiveness. Offsetting that loss would require a substantial investment in additional major combat forces and supply capabilities, and an expansion of existing base facilities. The costs involved in such enhancements could easily exceed $40 billion, probably making this more expensive than the other two alternatives. The chances are slim that the U.S. Congress would make such funding available, given the prevailing budgetary constraints.

## BUILDING NEW BASES: THE MARIANAS AND MICRONESIA

Although the Seventh Fleet and the Thirteenth Air Force could meet their combat responsibilities in Northeast Asia from bases in Japan and Guam, it would be very difficult for them to meet their deterrent and combat responsibilities in Southeast Asia and the Indian Ocean with anything like their present effectiveness so far from the site. The alternative suggestion that new facilities be constructed in the Marianas and in Micronesia (perhaps supplemented by an expansion of those in Guam) recommends itself for geographical reasons. Compared to relocation in Japan and Guam, it would bring the U.S. bases nearer the assigned operational areas in the South China Sea and the Indian Ocean and would significantly improve their ability to protect the sea and air routes through the chokepoints of the South China Sea and east of the Philippines.[7]

The United States has already leased land for military bases on Saipan and Tinian in the Marianas and on Palau, in Micronesia. The harbor at Palau could eventually host air strips that could be expanded to absorb the forces now based in the Philippines.

Palau is about 600 miles east of the Philippines, and relocating some facilities there would not diminish their effectiveness as much as relocating them in Japan and Guam. Nonetheless, maintaining present effectiveness would still require more forces than are needed for the current Philippine-based operations. Moreover, operations in the South China Sea would require transit and overflight permission from the Philippine government if the most direct and efficient flight paths from Palau and the Marianas were to be used.

The bases in the Marianas and Micronesia, supplemented by expanded facilities in Guam, could give the forces required by missions in Northeast Asia the same efficiency they now have. The distance to Northeast Asia is about the same from Guam as from the Philippines. Bases in Palau would provide security for vessels sailing west from North America to the South China Sea, but interdiction in the South China Sea would remain a serious threat as long as the Soviet Union maintained bases in Vietnam—particularly if the Philippine government refused overflight and transit permission.

If U.S. bases in the Philippines were relocated in the Marianas and Micronesia, there would be a reduction in naval presence and on-station time in the Indian Ocean and Persian Gulf region. This could be offset only by an increase in logistical capacity in order to provide fleet support commensurate with that available through Subic Bay. Traveling the additional 600 miles from Palau to any site in the South China Sea or beyond would complicate the U.S. Navy's ability to augment its forward deployed forces quickly, or to sustain its combatants on station in a crisis.

### The Start-up Problems

Perhaps the greatest disability of this alternative is that, although the United States has undertaken a lease program that includes use of the port facilities on Saipan (177 acres) and Tinian (18,000 acres), as well as a live-fire impact area on the island of Farallon de Medirilla (206 acres), there are now no major facilities on either the Marianas or Palau. Moreover, the islands are very small and provide no construction materials or space to house construction crews or service personnel. All materials as well as daily supplies for the workers would have to be brought in. The population of the islands is so small that not only construction workers but also support and maintenance personnel for the bases once they are built would have to be immigrants.

Moving and construction costs would be very high. Building a naval base involves complicated and extensive marine construction that requires skilled crews and heavy, sophisticated machinery. The development of adequate naval facilities in the Marianas could take up to a decade or more, and in 1983 estimates of the cost for the first five years of construction stood at $3 to $4 billion.

Forces stationed on the newly constructed bases would have to be enlarged to offset the increased steaming and flight time required to reach the areas of operation. What the costs might be would depend on how closely the new bases were expected to match the capability of those in the Philippines. The services performed at Subic Bay range so wide and deep that their complete replication would probably be prohibitive in cost. Duplicating the vast storage complexes available at Subic would be very difficult. The two airfields on Tinian and those on Palau could probably be upgraded to meet the staging and combat launch needs of bomber, tanker, and airlift units, but it would be impossible to provide the terrain for seasoning aircrews to navigation responsibilities and electronic warfare that is now available at the Crow Valley Range in the Philippines.

## A Defensive Arc

The best arrangement for relocating the Philippine bases largely in the new facilities would probably involve the use of

Guam, Palau, Saipan, and Tinian in a defensive arc, with the construction of a major naval base on Palau where an attack carrier could be berthed. Facilities on Guam could be augmented, and the several airfields in the Marianas could be expanded to absorb the tactical fighter and airlift wings now based in the Philippines. Communications centers could be reconstructed either in Malakal Harbor in the Palau chain or in the Marianas.

With all this, the Seventh Fleet and the Thirteenth Air Force would still be a considerable distance from their area of primary responsibility. And even with a commitment to major investments in construction over perhaps more than a decade, the new facilities would not be able to duplicate fully the storage space, airfield apron parking, and wharfside services now available in the Philippines. Crew training, combat simulation, and recreational facilities would be considerably inferior.

A final problem is that both Palau and the new states in the Marianas have expressed an intention to maintain a "nuclear free" environment. Palau, which has negotiated a compact of free association with the United States, has adopted a constitutional proscription against nuclear weapons in its territory. It is therefore not clear whether a naval base at Palau could host nuclear-weapons-capable military combatants. To have to base such vessels and aircraft at Guam would significantly reduce the operational flexibility of the new bases.

## RELOCATING IN A NEW HOST NATION

The principal disability suffered by the two previous relocation options is that both the existing bases and the suggested new bases would be a considerable distance from the site of the principal security responsibilities of the Seventh Fleet and the Thirteenth Air Force. That disadvantage could be offset by negotiating for an alternate base location in or near the South China Sea. Such choices would include: one of the sovereign states of the Association of Southeast Asian Nations (ASEAN);

the southern provinces of the People's Republic of China; or the Republic of China on Taiwan.

## The ASEAN States—Singapore

Among ASEAN members, Singapore and Thailand appear to be the most likely candidates. The other three members besides the Philippines—Indonesia, Malaysia, and Brunei—have shown no public disposition to consider hosting U.S. military bases. Malaysia and Indonesia have officially favored regional non-alignment and neutralization, but Singapore has not been enthusiastic about this policy. Singapore's prime minister was disturbed by Australia's decision, in 1973, to withdraw its military forces from the city-state. That coupled with Britain's decision to withdraw its forces west of the Suez left Singapore with the conviction that only the United States would serve as its bulwark against outside threats. During the U.S. involvement in Vietnam, U.S. naval vessels and military officers were welcomed in Singapore. The city-state became one of the service centers for U.S. operations in Indochina, and its authorities consistently supported the U.S. position.[8] The Seventh Fleet retains fueling privileges in Singapore. Singapore's location, too, commends it: it lies at the very mouth of the Malacca Strait, one of the major chokepoints between the Indian Ocean and the South China Sea.

But Singapore also suffers some major disadvantages as a potential base site. It could absorb only part of the forces now operating out of Subic Bay or Clark Field. Available space is very limited, and facilities provided for the Seventh Fleet would be very circumscribed. Storage of fuel, equipment, and ordnance could not begin to compare with that at Subic Bay. Little if any space would be available for air operations. Without airspace and with limited training facilities, the Republic of Singapore Air Force itself has had to use training areas available in other countries. In fact, Singapore has a permanent detachment of airmen at Clark Air Base, where they are trained at U.S. facilities. Additional training goes on in Australia and Thailand. Tengah, the main airfield in Singapore, is not large and could probably handle only three C-5 or five C-141 airlift aircraft at a time.

Singapore does have excellent commercial ship repair facilities, but they service ships of many nations—including the Soviet Union. The commercial use of the facilities would make it difficult to assure priority servicing of U.S. naval vessels should the need arise—and the presence of Soviet ships and personnel would create a potentially serious security problem.

A base in Singapore would be well situated for the defense of the Indonesian Straits and routes west to the Indian Ocean. It would be less advantageously positioned for defending sea and air routes to U.S. facilities in Guam, Okinawa, and farther east. Soviet forces in Vietnam could threaten interdiction, or at least complicate U.S. security planning for the entire South China Sea region, in the event of conflict.

Most troublesome, however, is the fact that in the past Singapore has been sensitive to external political pressures. In 1973, its government honored the Arab oil embargo against the West, a fact that raises the question whether the United States would have full use of Singapore's facilities in an international crisis.[9]

## Other ASEAN Considerations

Thailand offers more spacious naval and air base possibilities than Singapore, and during the Vietnam War it allowed the United States to use six of its military bases to stage operations in Indochina. But Bangkok has assumed a more neutral foreign policy since 1976. While relations between the two countries are perfectly correct and Washington has given Thailand's military substantial security assistance based on an executive understanding going back almost two decades, it is not likely that a large or permanent U.S. military force would be welcome on Thai soil.

Clearly, the nations of ASEAN view the presence of U.S. forces in the Philippines as a major stabilizing and security influence.[10] And all have misgivings about the increasing Soviet military presence in the region.[11] Nonetheless, most of the non-Communist nations of the South China Sea region prefer not to become inextricably involved in U.S. security arrangements. They would like to retain their "room for maneuver."[12] That any of them would be prepared to host a U.S. military base is doubtful at best.[13]

Relocating the bases in a new host nation would involve rental costs, the size of which would be hard to predict. If those costs were high, close congressional scrutiny of the proposal on both policy and fiscal grounds would be likely. While the costs might be less than building bases in the Marianas or Micronesia, the possibility that the host country would demand extensive U.S. foreign aid could not be ruled out. That would increase congressional resistance and render the outcome of such arrangements problematic.

### PRC and ROC Possibilities

Both the People's Republic of China (PRC) and the Republic of China on Taiwan (ROC) constitute potential host nations for U.S. bases. Both sites have advantages.

Bases located on Hainan Island (a large island, part of the PRC, that faces Vietnam across the Gulf of Tonkin) or on the PRC mainland or on Taiwan would have secure lines of communication with U.S. bases in Okinawa, Japan, Guam, and Hawaii. In times of crisis, bases located in either the PRC or the ROC could expect interactive support from bases to the east. Moreover, both Hainan and Taiwan are located on the major ship passageways from the South China Sea to Northeast Asia. Both offer staging areas that would contribute to the operational responsibilities of the Seventh Fleet and the Thirteenth Air Force in both the South China Sea region and Northeast Asia. While their location would be less advantageous than that of Singapore or Thailand for protecting the Indonesian chokepoints, bases on Hainan or Taiwan would be better located to neutralize Soviet forces in Vietnam and Kampuchea. In interdicting the threat from those bases, the forces from staging areas on Hainan or Taiwan would suppress the potential threat to the Indonesian waterways.

### The People's Republic of China

The establishment of U.S. facilities in the People's Republic of China large and complex enough to absorb the naval and air forces currently located in the Philippines would require very substantial investment. Although the PRC has developed some naval facilities on Hainan, its Southern Fleet is based not on Hainan but in Zhangjiang on the mainland. Hainan does have bases for naval aircraft; they provided air cover for the 1974 amphibious invasion of the Paracels.

Most of the PRC's ship servicing, repair, and construction is conducted in shipyards farther north, in Canton and Shanghai. Shanghai hosts a fourth of the PRC's building and repair yards and is the most important site for naval ship construction.[14] While these facilities are technologically backward, best suited for the construction and repair of relatively small, unsophisticated vessels, it is clear that low-cost and efficient shipyard workers would be available in the PRC for the ship services required by U.S. naval vessels.[15]

In all probability, any arrangement whereby the U.S. Navy was able to use facilities in the PRC would involve a relatively wide separation of actual port facilities and shipyard and dry-dock servicing. Space and airfield facilities would probably be at a premium, given the high population density along the coast.

While relocating U.S. bases on the Chinese mainland is technically feasible and would probably be relatively cost-effective, it appears unlikely that Beijing is prepared to consider such a possibility. While Washington has spoken vaguely of some sort of "security relationship" between the United States and the People's Republic of China, Beijing has insisted that such a relationship is not in the offing. Since 1980, Beijing has made it clear that it wishes to remain "equidistant" from both the Soviet Union and the United States in a posture it identifies as "foreign policy independence."[16]

The Communist Chinese have perfectly comprehensible reasons for not wishing to become directly involved in the forward basing of U.S. military forces in East Asia. As a consequence,

Beijing has been more than coy in allowing U.S. naval vessels to pay port calls to Chinese cities. It has used such visits in an apparent effort to influence its relations with the Soviet Union— rather than as a preliminary to negotiations for U.S. access to bases on PRC soil.[17]

### Sino-Soviet Relations

The leaders of the PRC recognize that to exploit their role in a three-cornered relationship with Moscow and Washington, they must not identify too closely with either. If Beijing wishes to be courted, she must remain coy.

The results are quite apparent. Since the death of Konstantin Chernenko in March 1985, the Soviets have shown considerable solicitude for PRC sensibilities. For the first time in two decades, the Soviet Communist Party extended official greetings to its Chinese counterpart. The Chinese reciprocated by addressing the new Soviet leader, Mikhail Gorbachev, as "Comrade." Gorbachev in turn urged that both countries "continue to heighten their level of dialogue, jointly work to reduce differences, and make progress in a wide scope of areas."[18]

By the beginning of 1985, the two countries had concluded a five-year economic pact calculated to increase bilateral trade by 22 per cent that year and 400 per cent by the end of the decade. Moscow now rarely if ever alludes to the PRC as a member of an "anti-Soviet alliance," and the Communist Chinese no longer refer to the Soviet Union as "social imperialist."[19] Relations between the two Communist giants remain something less than cordial, however, and very few analysts anticipate a Sino-Soviet rapprochement that would approach the intimate association of the 1950s. Nonetheless, it is clear that Beijing intends to avoid provoking Moscow.

Aside from its desire to exploit its position in the triangular relationship, Beijing is fully aware that the Soviet forces deployed along the Sino-Soviet border are so far superior to the PRC forces that any active anti-Soviet initiatives would be ill advised. Soviet armored forces, mobile infantry, tactical and strategic nuclear capabilities, and air power are overwhelmingly superior to anything the Communist Chinese People's Liberation Army can deploy; Mao Zedong's successors have therefore shown prudence and remarkable restraint.[20] For Beijing even to consider providing basing facilities for U.S. forces would be to invite incalculable Soviet response.

During the tensions of 1969, the People's Republic of China engaged Soviet forces in fire fights. The Soviet forces proceeded to savage the ill-equipped Chinese—and the Soviet forces involved were from units below the level of combat readiness. The lesson was well learned. Since that time, the PRC has diverted its energies and limited financial resources away from defense expenditures and from direct confrontation with the USSR, and has invested in overall economic development instead. The consequence has been a modest rapprochement with the Soviet Union, from which Beijing expects to purchase productive equipment to refurbish facilities installed with Soviet assistance more than three decades ago. Replacement parts and new equipment can be purchased at far more attractive prices from the Soviet Union than state-of-the-art equipment could be purchased from the industrially advanced Western powers.[21]

Finally, there are signs that the People's Republic of China is concerned about its future in the region. As we saw earlier, Beijing has tendered claims that cover the entire surface of the South China Sea. Its increasing emphasis on development of its Southern Fleet, as well as the development of a substantial blue-water capability for its combat vessels, suggests that the PRC is preparing to undertake initiatives in the area should that become necessary to defend its interests as Beijing sees them.[22] The presence of U.S. naval and air forces on mainland Chinese soil could be a major hindrance.

It is extremely unlikely, then, that Beijing would countenance the relocation of the U.S. Philippine bases on Chinese soil. U.S. forces clearly serve to restrain Soviet aggressiveness in the South China Sea and along the PRC's southern coastline. But their presence also serves to reduce Beijing's policy independence in the South China Sea.

## The Republic of China on Taiwan

Across the Taiwan Strait, the Nationalist Chinese have a fundamentally different relationship with the United States and have considered the Soviet Union an adversary at least since the end of the Second World War.

The Republic of China on Taiwan is the fifth largest trading partner of the United States; annual bilateral trade is around $22 billion. The ROC is market-governed, anti-Communist, and tendentially democratic.[23] It has supported U.S. initiatives in East Asia since 1949 and remains steadfastly in what Taipei identifies as the "democratic camp." Authorities in Taipei have every economic, political, and security reason to associate with the United States and the other advanced industrial democracies. The United States and Japan are its two principal trading partners, and its security remains largely dependent on the continued if unofficial support provided by Washington.

Since the end of the civil war in China in 1949, Beijing has insisted upon "reunification of the motherland"—that is, Taipei's surrender of any claim to sovereignty, and its readiness to submit to the dominance of Beijing. The PRC has been equally insistent that should Taipei refuse to submit, the issue will ultimately be resolved by force.

In this context of threat, the support of the United States is critical to the survival of the ROC. The Carter administration withdrew recognition from the ROC in 1978, but since then official Washington has regularly reaffirmed its concern with the peace and stability of the Taiwan Strait region. The Taiwan Relations Act of 1979 affirmed that "peace and stability in the area are in the political, security, and economic interests of the United States" and that "any effort to determine the future of Taiwan by other than peaceful means" would be a matter "of grave concern to the United States."[24]

Despite the severing of formal diplomatic relations, therefore, the United States remains a major, if informal, security partner of the Republic of China on Taiwan.[25] Taipei is, as a consequence, very responsive to U.S. interests throughout Asia.

Without question, the ROC would welcome U.S. forces to facilities on its territory. The presence of U.S. naval and air units would secure the island against aggression from without—specifically from the armed forces of the PRC. The security created by the U.S. presence would foster a stability that would make the island still more attractive to foreign investors; it would reduce domestic criticism of the Chiang Ching-kuo regime; and it would offset the present necessity of devoting about 10 per cent of the island's GNP to defense.

## The ROC Facilities

Prior to 1979, the United States and the Republic of China on Taiwan had had a security relationship for three decades. Units of the Seventh Fleet used facilities on the island, and elements of the Thirteenth Air Force were stationed on airfields there as part of the archipelagic deployment of U.S. forces from Japan through Okinawa and Taiwan to the Philippines. The Chinese on Taiwan serviced U.S. naval combatants and jet aircraft, and during the Vietnam conflict undertook major maintenance and repair of both naval vessels and aircraft. Most of the ROC's own military equipment, moreover, is of U.S. origin, and the largest combatants in the Nationalist Chinese Navy—its destroyers and frigates—are transfers from the U.S. Navy. Almost all the aircraft in service with the ROC Air Command are of U.S. design and, in part, of U.S. manufacture.

Consequently, the Taiwanese labor force includes a significant number of skilled workers who have had long experience with U.S. naval combatants, aircraft, armor, missiles, artillery, and small arms. As an industrialized nation, the ROC maintains an international fleet of air carriers that require maintenance and servicing, and the skills involved here are transferable to the advanced equipment of the U.S. armed forces. The few skills missing among Chinese workers on Taiwan (e.g., maintenance and repair of nuclear propulsion systems) can readily be supplied by special training.

The ROC Navy maintains extensive repair and refit facilities in various ports on the island. Major repair yards are located at

Kaohsiung and Tsoying in southern Taiwan, with secondary facilities at Keelung in the north. The capabilities of Taiwanese repair yards and construction facilities have been well demonstrated by the major retrofitting and modifications they have done on the destroyers, frigates, and fast attack craft now in the ROC Navy.[26]

The naval facilities on Taiwan are supplemented by a prospering commercial shipbuilding industry, with the twelfth largest facilities in the world. Its yards have built bulk carriers of over 100,000 tons displacement, and plans have been completed for vessels twice that large. The Kaohsiung yard of the China Shipbuilding Corporation has built highly sophisticated, automated, and computerized oil tankers of over 400,000 tons. The Taiwan Machinery Company has fabricated marine propulsion units for these vessels and has the capacity for producing metallurgically sophisticated vessel components.[27]

The port facilities in Taiwan are substantial by world standards. In 1984, for example, Kaohsiung handled 1.5 million twenty-foot-equivalent units of cargo, and was therefore the fifth largest container port in the world. In 1984, the ports of Taiwan handled over 76 million metric tons of cargo on over 33,000 meters of wharf. That, coupled with the availability of more than 200 cranes, thirty-four barges, and seventy-two tugs, assures a capacity for berthing and servicing naval vessels up to and including cruisers.

Dry docks in Kaohsiung, Tsoying, and Keelung can handle vessels as large as destroyers, but major hull repairs to larger vessels, such as a large-deck carrier, would have to be done in Japan or Hawaii. Removing aircraft from carriers in Taiwanese ports would be a rather complicated and somewhat risky operation involving cranes and barges. Given Taiwan's population density and industrial development, storage space for fuel, petroleum, lubricants, and ordnance would be at a premium. On the positive side, the communications and transportation infrastructure of the island is well developed, and adequate supplies of electrical energy are assured.

Substantial live-fire training zones available on Taiwan compare favorably with those at Crow Valley in the Philippines. The

Taiwanese ranges can accommodate naval, artillery, and small-arms fire, as well as aircraft strafing and bombing runs. The availability of land and sea space for combat simulation and joint forces training adds to Taiwan's attractiveness.

Taiwan's air bases, with some expansion of facilities, could probably absorb both the tactical fighter and airlift wings now stationed in the Philippines. The ROC Air Command has modern air support and ground facilities for its own force of more than 400 aircraft. There is space on Taiwan for some considerable expansion of airfield facilities, particularly in the less developed areas. Unlike Japan, Taiwan would present little public resistance to such developments.

### Geographical Advantages

The island and its bases are ideally situated to control sea traffic in both the Taiwan Strait and the Bashi Channel—through which most of the vessels from Europe and the Middle East must pass to reach Soviet and non-Communist Northeast Asia. The island and its bases are less well situated than Singapore or Thailand for controlling ship passage through the Malacca Strait or the other Indonesian chokepoints. Nonetheless, Taiwan bases would provide facilities closer to the areas of primary responsibility for the Seventh Fleet and the Thirteenth Air Force than any existing U.S. bases or any new construction in the Marianas or Micronesia. Furthermore, bases could be more easily defended in Taiwan than in Singapore or Thailand, since there would be no Soviet bases between them and major U.S. facilities further east.

All in all, Taiwan bases would be an attractive alternative to the bases in the Philippines. The cost of relocation would be manageable, and certainly no more than the cost of any alternative. It is very unlikely that Taipei would attempt to negotiate a high rental fee since the presence of U.S. forces would contribute to the security, stability, and subsequent economic attractiveness of the island. Finally, because the bases would be closer to the major mission sites of the Seventh Fleet, little enhancement of forces would be required to make a military presence in the area equivalent to the current one.

### The PRC Constraint

The major constraint upon an effort to relocate the U.S. Philippine military bases on Taiwan would be political. Since the mid-1970s, the United States has assiduously cultivated ties with Beijing. Clearly, Washington feels that the PRC serves U.S. interests by forcing the Soviet Union to deploy perhaps as much as a third of its conventional and strategic forces along the Sino-Soviet border, thereby assuring their unavailability for any adventures elsewhere against the industrialized democracies.[28] The visit of Secretary of Defense Harold Brown to Communist China in 1980 (immediately after the Soviet invasion of Afghanistan) established the groundwork for a security connection between Washington and Beijing. Subsequent visits of Secretary of Commerce Malcolm Baldrige in August 1983 and Secretary of Defense Caspar Weinberger a month later were signs of a growing relationship.[29]

A number of influential studies prepared by U.S. government agencies and by foreign policy consultants since the mid-1970s recommended the pursuit of a security tie and resulted in a "detailed plan for establishing a far-reaching military relationship with China in an incremental, step-by-step manner."[30] The PRC's defense minister, Zhang Aiping, and its naval commander, Liu Huaqing, visited the United States (in June 1984 and November 1985), and in 1985 the U.S. secretary of the Navy, the chairman of the Joint Chiefs of Staff, and the Air Force chief of staff went separately to Communist China.[31] Zbigniew Brzezinski, Alexander Haig, and Caspar Weinberger have all argued that a U.S.-PRC security relationship would "contain" the Soviet Union and "counter Soviet expansionism in East Asia."[32]

As a consequence, the PRC has been considered a major security interest for the United States, and good relations between the two countries have been given priority. Beijing has made it very clear that the attempt to reestablish the kind of security relationship involved in maintaining military bases on Taiwan would create problems in the U.S.-PRC relationship.[33]

Ultimately, the real question becomes: how important is the PRC connection to the U.S. attempt to contain Soviet expansionism? There would be inevitable tradeoffs involved in all the options for moving the military bases now in the Philippines. Of the alternatives available for the forward basing of U.S. naval and air forces in the West Pacific, the Republic of China on Taiwan is probably the best. Would the operational, political, and financial advantages offset the real and perceived costs entailed in alienating Beijing? Would those costs be greater than the costs of the other options?

Answers to questions like these require an analysis far more extensive than can be undertaken here,[34] but several things can be said. (1) The difficulties that have attended relations between Moscow and Beijing and that make the PRC a security asset to the United States are the product of factors with a long history; they are unlikely to be overcome in the foreseeable future. (2) It is therefore unlikely that relations between the two Communist countries will go beyond being proper, and the Soviet Union will probably maintain the current level of defense capabilities along the Sino-Soviet border. (3) The Soviet Union is likely to enter into fairly extensive political and trade relations with the PRC, but a major drawdown of Soviet forces from East Asia is very unlikely as long as the United States and its allies maintain a credible force structure there. (4) Because of all this, the United States need not concern itself unduly with Beijing's sensibilities. Nothing Washington does is likely either to throw Beijing into the arms of Moscow or to precipitate a withdrawal of Soviet forces from East Asia.

It is in the PRC's interests that the United States provide a counterweight to the Soviet Union in the West Pacific and the South China Sea region. Although the Communist Chinese do not anticipate overt conflict with the Soviet Union, the Soviet and Vietnamese threat remains very real for Beijing.[35] The U.S. military presence in the region reduces the risk of Soviet or

Vietnamese adventure. Beijing has already expressed concern that the United States might be forced to leave the Philippines.

Beijing, then, given its interests, can be expected to enter into a modest rapprochement with Moscow that might prompt cosmetic force reductions along the Sino-Soviet border—and a major reduction in histrionics. But under almost no circumstances would Beijing be likely to sever all relations with the United States. In addition to its role as a counterweight to the Soviet Union in Asia, and a constraint on Soviet and Vietnamese initiatives, the United States remains one of the major sources of advanced technology for the backward economy of the PRC.

For its part, Washington appears ill disposed to challenge Beijing on any substantive issue, and particularly the sensitive issue of Taiwan. U.S. China policy appears to have a momentum now that would make a basing arrangement with the ROC most unlikely. Only if Beijing continues its "independent" foreign policy, voting (as it does) against the United States in the United Nations almost as often as the Soviet Union, objecting to U.S. policy almost everywhere in the world, and supporting anti-American posturing among the less developed nations, might some change be forthcoming in Washington's accommodative policy. Should such a change take place, the evidence suggests that U.S. security policy would benefit, allowing Washington greater latitude in its tactical maneuvering. Washington would pursue a policy as "independent" as that of Beijing. Part of the renewed independence would be an arrangement with Taipei to allow the transfer of U.S. forces to new bases in Taiwan should Manila make such a move necessary.

## THE BALANCE SHEET

Under the best circumstances, the United States would suffer considerable degradation of its operational and forward-projection capabilities in Southeast Asia and the Indian Ocean region if forced to withdraw from the Philippines. No single adequate substitute for those bases presents itself. The best alternative available is relocation to the island of Taiwan and associated territories, but that alternative has considerable political costs. The United States could expect its relationship with Beijing to suffer substantially as a consequence.

Moreover, bases on Taiwan could not provide all the facilities available in the Philippines. Attack and multi-purpose carriers could not be dry-docked at facilities in Taiwan, storage space would be circumscribed, and the overall space for training and combat seasoning would not be as ample as that in the Philippines.

Other alternatives open to the United States either are very costly, entail operational impairments, or both. Absorbing the forces presently based in the Philippines would overload U.S. bases in Japan, Okinawa, and Guam. Moreover, it would position the forces at critical distances from the South China Sea and the Indian Ocean. Bases nearer to the operational sites would have to be built—costing billions and requiring about a decade for construction.

Given the prevailing world situation, it is greatly in the interest of the United States to try to help stabilize the volatile situation in the Philippines. The U.S. capabilities dependent on access to Philippine bases serve the interests of all the non-Communist nations in the region, and may well serve those of the People's Republic of China as well.

# 6

# *The Elements of Policy*

THE INTERESTS OF THE United States and the other industrialized democracies are intimately associated with the fate of
the Philippines. Access to the military bases there, a matter of
U.S. concern since before the First World War, has been a
preoccupation for at least five U.S. administrations during the
past four decades.[1] The Philippine republic is one of the oldest
democracies in Asia. Its economy remains essentially market
governed. The republic is one of a group of productive com-
munities that could well constitute an economic "boom belt" by
the end of the present century. Now that the socialist systems of
Eastern Europe and Asia have thoroughly discredited themselves by their singularly poor economic performances and their
massive derogations of civil and political rights, countries like
the Philippines could serve as a model of development for the
Third World.

In the ongoing struggle between open and closed societies, it
is important that those polities that are open, or have the
potential for openness, not only survive but prosper. So many
difficulties afflict the Philippines that its prospects even for
survival are not good. Its economic, military, and political
problems are so threatening that there may not be much time left
for their resolution. The collapse of the present government
could be the preamble to a Communist succession. That would
not only bring a dark night to the people of the Philippines but
would seriously undermine the future prospects of the other
ASEAN nations, and indeed of all Asia.

A radical government in Manila, or a coalition government
that incorporated a substantial number of radical members,
would no doubt mean an end to the security relationship with the
United States and the loss of U.S. access to the Philippine

93

bases. A diminished U.S. military presence in the region would contribute to the Soviet Union's plans for expansion into the South China Sea and the South Pacific. At present, the U.S. deployment in the Philippines constitutes a critical variable in any Soviet calculations. However well entrenched the Soviet Union might become in the South Pacific, its supply lines and freedom of movement always remain jeopardized by the mobile presence of U.S. forces. Without access to the Philippine bases, however, the U.S. forces would no longer be readily available. Their absence could very well influence the responses made by the small nations of the South Pacific to Soviet blandishments.

To maintain its presence in the area, the United States will have to assist the Republic of the Philippines through its present time of trouble, until a reasonable measure of economic growth and political stability foreclose the possibility of the accession of radicals to power. The United States, of course, can neither ensure an adequate rate of real economic growth nor impose stability, but it can make significant contributions to both.


## THE ECONOMIC PROBLEMS


As we have seen, the economy of the Philippines collapsed into negative growth. The Aquino administration must do many things to try to restore some measure of vitality and growth. There has been some talk in Manila of "privatizing the econ-omy," aggressively pursuing land reform, dismantling govern-ment-controlled monopolies and monopsonies (especially in the sugar and coconut industries), selling off the non-performing assets that are a legacy of mismanagement, reducing the govern-ment bureaucracy (which employs about 1.2 million persons), liberalizing the export sector, reducing the tariff protection for noncompetitive domestic industry, attracting foreign invest-ment, and imposing a more effective direct and progressive tax system.[2] The goals are to stabilize the exchange rate for the peso, control inflation, lower interest rates to the 15–20 per cent range, stimulate agricultural production, and promote a mini-mum rate of real growth of 2 per cent in the immediate future.

To achieve any of these purposes will require not only massive short-term economic assistance to provide sufficient capital to maintain domestic and export production but an inflexible commitment to all aspects of the program. Firm resolve is required, because every step will cost the Aquino government some support. Reducing the size of the government bureaucracy will cost individuals their livelihood; liberalizing the tariff structure will cause the collapse of an entire collection of non-competitive domestic industries; imposing an effective tax system will alienate those who have never been taxed before.

Those affected are almost certain to oppose the program. They could aggregate their complaints through membership in existing "anti-imperialist" and "nationalist" political organizations. Allowing domestic industries to succumb to foreign competition, soliciting foreign investment, undertaking to build foreign exchange reserves through a program of export sales— these policies have all been characterized by "nationalists" and "anti-imperialists" as "neocolonialist," and their sponsors as "lackeys of imperialism."

The economic program advertised by the Aquino government is essentially the one long advocated by the international financial institutions that have provided the bulk of the loans to the Philippine government. The United States had proposed similar reforms to the Marcos government, and academics such as Gustav Ranis had long advocated them.[3] The Marcos administration, well aware of the recommendations, had made some desultory attempts to implement them.[4] But it was evident to Marcos that determined efforts at implementation would have palpable political costs. As the Marcos administration's control over the nation became increasingly tenuous, pursuing the reforms could only have reduced its capacity to survive. Ferdinand Marcos could not afford to alienate any more elements in his narrowing constituency.

The Aquino administration will face much the same problem. The major difference at the moment is that Corazon Aquino appears to have the genuine support of a substantial number of Filipinos. Should her administration seriously attempt to implement the proposed economic program, however, defections and opposition can be expected. Unless positive results are forth-coming in the relatively near term, political problems will begin to accumulate. The response of the Aquino government might be to seek recourse in an alternative program of economic rehabilitation.

### The Alternative: Turning Inward

Such an alternative already exists. As we have seen, national-ists and anti-imperialists have long been its proponents. It would include an "inward directed" economic strategy, with tariff defenses for local industry, default on external debt, a "self-reliant" program of development, and an appeal to socialist and Third World nations for material aid and support. Many of the leaders of the anti-Marcos organizations paid at least lip service to such a program when they were in the opposition. It had clear appeal to a substantial number of Filipinos at the time—and probably will have again in the absence of a rapid improvement in the economy.

If positive results do not begin to appear quickly to provide political support for the proposed open and export-oriented economic program, a substantial movement to the left can be anticipated. Many followers of Corazon Aquino gave ample evidence of their readiness to make that move while they were in active opposition to Marcos. A failure of the "neocolonialist" program to produce quick results would regenerate and rein-force that disposition. Many among Aquino's original followers are prepared to appeal to "nationalist" and "anti-imperialist" sentiment among the urban intellectuals, disaffected labor groups, producers for the home market, impoverished urban squatters, and the destitute in the countryside. They could count on the support of all those "human rights advocates" who for years have identified the United States as the source of all the ills that afflict Filipinos, and all those "civil libertarians" who seek to settle scores with the Philippine military.

The temporary coalition of political forces that rendered the post-Marcos Philippines a "friend" of the United States is not stable, and unless the Aquino administration can produce results quickly, it will find itself under pressure to assume anti-American and more "anti-imperialist" postures.

### Some Means of U.S. Support

The United States can do very little to influence developments in the Philippines directly, but certain measures might provide collateral support for the Aquino administration and the current coalition. The most obvious is substantial economic aid. While it is clear that the suggestion of the new Philippine ambassador to the United States, Emmanuel Pelaez,[5] that Washington undertake a "New Marshall Plan" to salvage his nation's economy could hardly be taken seriously by a budget-sensitive Congress, it is evident that much more than the $650 million thus far made available to Manila will be needed. The issues involved are so critical that the United States should be, and appears to be, prepared to put together "a major package of financial assistance from free world resources."[6]

The United States has already encouraged greater commitment by multilateral financial institutions to provide loans and credits to the Philippines, reschedule debt repayment, and provide additional contingency funds. Washington has considerable influence with the International Monetary Fund and can expedite the release of the last portion ($225 million) of the December 1984 standby credit facility. That would release a further $350 million made available from 483 foreign creditor banks. This together with the planned advances of $100 million from the Asian Development Bank and about $750 million from the World Bank in the immediate future materially assists the Philippine recovery.[7]

The United States could also urge the Japanese to release the $287 million in loans originally committed to the Philippines through the Overseas Cooperation Fund but delayed because of an investigation into improprieties by the Marcos administration. All this would provide not only material support for the devastated Philippine economy but also hard evidence of U.S. assistance and concern.

To provide further support, Washington should resist mount-

ing protectionist demands by U.S. producers, continue to increase the sugar quota (which was drastically reduced over the
past several years because of a glut of sugar), renew the bilateral
textile agreement that provides Philippine exports access to the
U.S. market, and enhance Philippine participation in the Gener-
alized System of Preferences (GSP), which would give Philippine exports to the United States preferential treatment. Short-
term credits for U.S. firms that purchase Philippine products,
and insurance for U.S. private investors in the Philippines
through the Overseas Private Investment Corporation, would
contribute to growth possibilities in the islands. At some point,
Washington should consider a bilateral trade treaty in order to
give some stability and predictability to the export trade of the
Philippines.

Efforts of this kind could be implemented with a Department
of Commerce mission to Manila to suggest ways to increase
Philippine exports to the United States. Other potentially useful
undertakings might include a program initiated by the U.S.
government that would arrange visits to the Philippines by
venture capitalists and representatives of major U.S. corporations and banks, with the purpose of stimulating bilateral activity, and a special presidential commission to report on short-
term and long-term initiatives that the U.S. government and
private sector could take to strengthen the Philippine economy.[8]
Such measures might prove very helpful as confidence-building
steps, and could serve to undercut the anti-American sentiment
that is sometimes more than latent among Aquino's followers.

All this would be a small investment, considering the potential
costs involved in the failure of the current efforts at reform.
Without an economic revival, a suppression or dissipation of the
insurrection that threatens both the Aquino administration and
U.S. interests in the Philippines seems unlikely. Without economic recovery, a resurfacing of all the anti-U.S. posturing that
preceded the February 1986 coup can be expected. That, together with the prevalence of armed insurrection, could augur a
radical turn to the left in Manila.

Should anything like this happen, the first evidence of the
change would probably include an effort by the government in
Manila to undercut the balancing influence of the military. The

military represents a continuity in Philippine politics that augurs well for U.S. interests. Any effort to neutralize it would signal a major shift in Manila's disposition toward the United States and an opening to the left.

## THE MILITARY PROBLEMS

The Aquino government came to power as a direct result of military intervention. In return, both Enrile and Ramos retained their positions. The military brought a perspective on government and foreign policy compatible with the economic and security interests of the United States. It is the presence of the military among the leaders of the present government that provides the real basis for the American conviction that the "people's revolution" of Corazon Aquino served the interests of both the Philippine people and the United States.

Present circumstances in the Philippines do not augur well for suppression of the New People's Army (NPA). The guerrilla forces deployed by the Philippine Communist Party are mobile and formidable enough to constitute a present danger to the survival of the republic. Since the advent of the Aquino administration, the NPA has continued its attacks against both civilian and military targets. More than a thousand persons were killed through NPA activities during the first 100 days of the Aquino incumbency.[9] Whatever the intentions of Corazon Aquino in her call for a ceasefire, the NPA is operating from a position of strength, and its leadership has announced that it will not surrender its current advantages for anything less than participation in the government (something President Aquino has insisted would not be possible), the dismissal of the leaders of the military, and an abrogation of the U.S.-Philippine Military Bases Agreement.[10]

The military has insisted that while a political solution to the Communist insurrection should be pursued, the NPA leadership is unlikely to negotiate seriously unless it is defeated in the field.[11] That defeat would require counterinsurgency forces with greater mobility, more effective firepower, better communica-

tions facilities, and higher institutional motivation than the
Armed Forces of the Philippines have possessed to date.

### Underfunding the Military

Almost all the disabilities that afflict the military are due to
budgetary restraints. The AFP has had to work with one of the
most meager defense budgets in all Asia. For decades the
Philippine government has allocated only about 1 per cent of the
gross national product (GNP) to defense. In comparison, Singapore's military budget consumes 5.8 per cent of its GNP; those
of Malaysia and Indonesia, 3.8 per cent; and Thailand's, 3.5 per
cent.

This translates into about $1,190 per soldier in the Philippines,
$5,730 per soldier in Thailand, $6,350 per soldier in Malaysia,
and $12,000 per soldier in Singapore. The Armed Forces of the
Philippines suffer inadequacies in transport equipment, communications adjuncts, armored mobility, training, pay, and subsistence supplements. These deficiencies affect morale and impair the combat readiness of troops in the field. All this hinders
the counterinsurgency effort.

Because of the economic problems, in real terms the funding
available for military expenditures in 1984 was only 80 per cent
of that available in 1972. In that time the armed forces, including
the Constabulary and the Civilian Home Defense forces, have
more than doubled in personnel.[12]

### Need for U.S. Military Aid

In the short term, therefore, the Philippine military will need
substantial assistance from the United States if it is to overcome
its most serious disabilities. That assistance will have to come
through both direct grants and concessional loans. The funds
will probably have to exceed the levels of military aid currently
anticipated in Washington.

In the near future, if the situation does not dramatically
change, it will probably be advisable for the United States to

undertake some special training responsibilities with the Armed Forces of the Philippines. In the past, U.S. and Philippine troops have occasionally engaged in joint exercises as part of mutual security arrangements. In May 1983, for example, 14,000 U.S. troops and Philippine marines undertook a twenty-day amphibious training exercise in Aurora Province on Luzon. Smaller exercises had taken place the year before and in 1980. Joint military exercises and training seminars involving pilots from the Singaporean and Philippine air forces are conducted by the U.S. Air Force at Clark Air Base, and military intelligence is shared by all the armed forces of the ASEAN community through the Pacific Armies Management Seminar, conducted under the auspices of the U.S. military command in the Philippines.

Special counterinsurgency training of Philippine troops would expand upon these programs, following as precedents the military assistance and training provided by the U.S. military command to the Philippine armed forces in the late 1940s and 1950s. U.S. assistance at that time contributed to the defeat of the Communist-led Hukbong Magpalaya ng Bayan (People's Liberation Army).[13] The twenty-eight battalions of counterinsurgency troops that succeeded in suppressing the Huk guerrillas were trained and armed by the U.S. military.[14]

While it seems evident that the ultimate defeat of the Communist insurrection will be contingent upon the self-sustained growth of the Philippine economy, the New People's Army must at least be contained until that growth commences. The alternative would be to allow the insurrectionists to increase their leverage over the central government, until by dint of concessions they could become arbiters in the nation's politics.

### The "Diokno Problem"

The leaders of the NPA have made it clear that to achieve a permanent ceasefire the Aquino government will have to make major concessions. Those concessions include, as we have seen, the dismissal of General Ramos as well as Juan Ponce Enrile.

Regrettably, the representatives chosen by President Aquino to negotiate with the NPA on these issues share the views of the late Jose Diokno, a longtime opponent of Enrile and Ramos and an acerbic critic of the Philippine armed services. As chairman of the Commission on Human Rights, Diokno had been charged with investigating and prosecuting persons he had long defamed. His successors will have to moderate their attacks if the military is not to be completely alienated.

The choice of Diokno to preside over negotiations with the NPA suggests something about the Aquino administration. Diokno had made his position eminently clear, and that position was accommodative. He shared the NPA's opposition to the military leadership of the nation. It is not hard to see, then, why the military felt the Aquino administration was not protecting its corporate interests. For the government to continue to pursue such policies could prove fatal. Signs of disaffection among the military increase.

One way to reduce the possibility of further deterioration in government-military relations is to defeat the NPA in the field as quickly as possible. There is every reason to believe that such a victory would allow the Aquino administration to reaffirm its ties with the Armed Forces of the Philippines.

The defeat of the NPA could probably be accomplished by the Philippine armed forces with U.S. military aid and enhanced training. However, the time left to pursue that outcome appears to be dwindling rapidly. U.S. intelligence estimates put the remaining time at two or three years. After that, the Communist insurrectionists will have achieved "strategic stalemate"—they will have fought the Philippine military to a standstill and will then be able to undertake the offensive.[15]

### Negotiating From Weakness

The Aquino government seems to have chosen to negotiate with the Communist insurgents from a position of weakness. Over the objections of the military, Aquino freed the jailed leadership of the revolutionary forces—who now travel the nation lecturing audiences about the imperatives of revolution.

This becomes comprehensible only when it is recalled that many in the anti-Marcos opposition had settled on a policy of reconciliation with the Philippine Communists years ago. In December 1984, almost the entire leadership of the Aquino political forces went on record as favoring the legalization of the insurrectionary Communist Party. The conviction seems to have been that the Communists had undertaken revolution specifically against the Marcos regime and with the advent of a "popular" government would surrender their weapons, seek peace, and pursue the "democratic path."

In that context, negotiations with the NPA appear to represent a serious political effort by the administration, and sending in sympathizers from the left to negotiate with the insurrectionists makes some kind of sense. Those who share Diokno's reservations about the role of the military in the country's politics also share similar objections to the presence of the U.S. military on Philippine soil. In fact, Diokno represented the views of the left-wing "moderates" when he crafted the Declaration of Principles for the Anti-Bases Coalition in 1983 that called for "immediate and unconditional removal of all U.S. bases and military installations in the Philippines," and "immediate abrogation" of the Military Bases Agreement and all related security accords with the United States.[16]

If the Aquino administration really believes that reconciliation with the revolutionaries of the NPA is possible, showing good faith by sending left-wing sympathizers as negotiators might make tactical sense. Perhaps the intention is not only to bring about a ceasefire but also to placate a sizable and articulate constituency on the left that has long impugned the military and advocated a general "anti-imperialist" policy with regard to the United States.

Corazon Aquino may, moreover, be exploiting an opportunity to weaken the position of the Philippine military leadership. Pursuing peace through negotiation seems eminently reasonable and allows her, rather than the military, to direct the course of events. Moreover, as long as negotiations continue she is not required to supply the armed forces with the enhanced budget that would both render them combat ready and increase the political potential of their leaders. Whatever the case, the current relationship of the Aquino administration to the NPA insurgents and their legal and semi-legal allies does not bode well either for the future of military-civilian collaboration in the Philippines or for U.S. economic and security interests.

## THE POLITICAL PROBLEMS

All these matters translate almost immediately into political expression. Since the public coup that brought her to power in February 1986, Corazon Aquino has not made very clear the political course she intends to follow. In her first year in office, she made herself the most powerful ruler in Philippine history. She took upon herself the power to issue decree legislation. She abolished the representative National Assembly. She had more than 14,000 local elective posts declared vacant, authorizing her then minister of local government, Aquilino Pimentel, to appoint "officers in charge" to replace fifty-five of seventy-four provincial governors, forty-eight of sixty city mayors, nearly half the mayors of towns, and hundreds of vice governors, vice mayors, provincial board members, and local councilmen.[17] She insisted on the resignation of Supreme Court justices and began reorganizing the Intermediate Appellate Court. She then called on fifty representatives to form a commission to draft a new constitution. In effect, Corazon Aquino has erected the most authoritarian government in the history of the Philippines—however "interim" that government may turn out to be.

Serious strains have appeared among the leaders of the coalition that forms the political base of the Aquino administration.[18] Members of Salvador Laurel's UNIDO have raised the most explicit objections. UNIDO received only six of the twenty ministerial posts in the new government, and when Aquino abolished the elective assembly, UNIDO lost the forty-nine seats its members had won in the 1984 elections. Pimentel's appointments of "officers in charge" to assume obligations of those elective posts abolished by Aquino were made largely from his own Philippine Democratic Party. When other members of the Aquino coalition objected, President Aquino curbed Pimentel's appointive power and revoked some of his appointments.

The Aquino coalition is a disunited collection of parties, special-interest groups, and individual political leaders. Policy pronouncements, as a consequence, appear indecisive and irresolute. Vice President and Foreign Minister Laurel has vacillated from his 1983 stand advocating immediate abrogation of the Military Bases Agreement and now favors maintaining the agreement at least until 1991, when the issue would be put to the voters. Aquino, in her first news conference as a candidate for president, announced that she would work steadfastly for removal of the U.S. bases.[19] Thereafter she modified her position and held that she would support the bases agreement until 1991, after which "all options" would be open.

As for economic policy, in 1983 Salvador Laurel announced an "alternative" to the program then being pursued by the Marcos administration. The policy Laurel proposed would "redirect the . . . colonial, export, import trade-oriented, and foreign-dominated and exploited economy into one . . . [that derived] its strength from a domestic market of 50 million Filipinos." The redirection would involve "reversing the policies" that had opened the Philippines to the "rapacious exploitation of foreign interests." This was to be done by rejecting the "trade and tariff liberalization policies" of the Marcos government, in order to provide "reasonable protection to domestically manufactured products."[20]

### Mixed Signals From Aquino

All this contradicts the main thrust of the present announced economic policies of the Aquino administration. But it is hard to determine how great a conflict there actually is, for the convictions of Corazon Aquino are not at all clear.

The "Unity Platform" that she put together with the counsel

of Lorenzo Tañada in December 1984 exudes the "anti-imperialist" sentiments that imply anti-Americanism and a redirection of
the national economy. The Unity Platform urged a "minimum
plank" requiring that Aquino's followers work to free the Philippines of "any form of economic, cultural, and political domination or interference by any government or any foreign power."
The platform went on to say that "all economic and financial
agreements, entered into, assumed, or guaranteed by the Marcos regime, will be subjected to public review." The platform
also asserted that "foreign military bases on Philippine territory
must be removed."[21]

All this sounds very much like the populist anti-imperialism of
the urban intellectuals who formed much of the cadre of the
"people's revolution" that brought Aquino to power. What
"political domination" and "interference" might mean in such a
context is impossible to say. That "all economic and financial
agreements" require review could suggest default on international loan obligations, or it could mean nothing at all. But the
removal of "foreign military bases" would seem to mean at least
that.

What we have in Corazon Aquino's preelection program, in
fact, is a collection of policy proposals that could mean different
things to different interpreters. There is a clear undercurrent of
"anti-imperialism" and the anti-Americanism that this notion
implies. All this allows the left—the NPA–Communist Party, its
"united front" adjuncts, and any and all fellow travelers—to
exploit any confusion and irresolution that surfaces in the policies of the administration.

The environment in which the Aquino administration must
operate is not conducive to maintaining a loose coalition of
groups and individuals that entertain disparate views on major
issues. Worse than that, within the coalition are a number of
persons in prominent positions whose convictions are threatening to essential U.S. interests. Jovito Salonga is serving as
chairman of the Commission on Good Government. He and his
Liberal Party, in a formal Fifteen Point Program, hold that the
Philippine people must "oppose . . . the continued presence of

military bases in the Philippines."[22] Rogaciano Mercado, until recently minister of public works, is a leader of an anti-bases organization that demonstrated outside Clark Air Base, demanding that the Philippines become "truly independent" by "denouncing the U.S. military presence in the Philippines."[23] Jaime Ongpin, minister of finance, was a convenor of the Unity Council of December 1984 whose platform included the now familiar demand that "foreign military bases on Philippine territory must be removed and no foreign military bases shall hereafter be allowed."[24] Ramon Mitra, minister of agriculture in the Aquino government, was a signatory to that declaration. Both inside and outside the present administration, all these persons are important political actors in the complex Philippine environment.

As we have seen, both President Aquino and Vice President Laurel[25] have in the past demanded the evacuation of the U.S. bases, though both have subsequently waffled on the issue. The administration still includes those who have consistently opposed the U.S. military presence. President Aquino has attempted to remove the most objectionable members of her cabinet in that regard, but it remains unclear whether the issue has been successfully defused. If it has not, U.S. interests will remain in jeopardy and the Philippine military may prove increasingly difficult for the Aquino administration to handle.

## A Coalition With the Left

The organized left in the Philippines has been consistent in opposing "imperialism." As we have seen, the views of a significant number of Philippine intellectuals are compatible with those of the radical left. In the general population there are enough persons sharing such views to provide 750,000 members for the left radical Movement of Philippine Farmers and for the May First Movement, the largest labor federation in the islands. Such persons supply the mass for the demonstrations that have shaken the Aquino government.

If the economic situation does not improve quickly, and if the influence of the military diminishes, an appeal to anti-foreign and anti-American sentiment would recommend itself to an insecure and politically divided leadership. Such a political devolution could bring the organized left into the government. The legalized Communist Party, having accommodated itself to the Aquino administration, would be in a position to enter into a coalition government. Such a coalition, involving a Communist Party with its own political army and its own "united front" adherents, could easily succeed to dominance—particularly if the leadership of the Armed Forces of the Philippines is sufficiently impaired.

Whatever else such a coalition might disagree on, there would be consensus on U.S. interests in the islands. The radical left, the left, and most of those groups Americans like to think of as "moderates" could easily agree on the necessity of circumscribing "imperialist" influence in the Philippines. U.S. economic and security interests would be the first casualties of any coalition dominated by the political left.

Such a coalition would appeal to that segment of the business community that would profit by insulation from the international trading system—those unable or unwilling to compete for foreign market shares, or to allow foreign products to compete with their own in the domestic market. As we saw previously, intellectuals, journalists, left-wing labor groups, alienated professionals, urban squatters, some of the unemployed, and "progressive" church groups would all be a part of such a constituency. All these groups have expressed at least some of the anti-U.S. sentiments that animate a substantial part of Corazon Aquino's "people's movement." Such groups were gradually drawn together and sustained by the insistence that the Marcos era represented a "U.S.-Marcos dictatorship," and that the U.S. presence in the Philippines is a manifestation of "neocolonialism" and a major instrument of oppression and exploitation.

All these sentiments have been bruited so long in the Philippines that there is now a hard core of politically active persons—with membership in almost every organization in the islands—who can be expected to support any coalition committed to anti-U.S. initiatives. An Aquino administration disspirited by its failure to restart the economy, or to solve the problem of armed insurrection, would be increasingly pressured to move to the left in order to pick up the support that could be purchased by an overt anti-Americanism.

### The Military and the Government

The United States must do whatever it can to prevent this from happening. The Aquino administration still anticipates major assistance from Washington, both in direct economic aid and in the exercise of U.S. influence with world financial institutions on behalf of the Philippines. As a consequence, the anti-American grumblings that for years typified the "moderate" opposition to Marcos are rarely heard at the moment. Corazon Aquino has made an obvious effort to emphasize the positive role of the Philippine military in the task of national reconstruction, and she has alluded to the fact that other foreign bases in the region might warrant the continued presence of the U.S. military in the archipelago.[26] Representatives of the Philippine military in the Aquino government serve as a counterweight to representatives of the left and the "anti-imperialists." Pro-Western elements would be expected to collect around the anti-radical military.

At the same time, the military has become increasingly restive under presidential orders to minimize contact engagements with the Communist insurgents. While the Armed Forces of the Philippines are restrained, the rural guerrillas have continued to press the initiative. In several engagements soldiers of the Philippine security forces have been ambushed. The military has communicated its increasing unwillingness to comply with what appear to be counterproductive restrictions that favor their opponents. For example, it released figures showing that the insurgents increased their numbers substantially during the first 100 days of the Aquino administration.[27]

Should the Aquino government drift to the left, the military may find itself driven to intervene—and the issue of the Communist insurgency may be the concern around which the military and its civilian allies in the business community, the church, and the general public could collect. The consequence might well be the major confrontation that was avoided by the coup in February 1986. Some evidence suggests that military leaders remain uneasy about the presence of what they consider leftist elements in the Aquino administration.[28] Neither faction, left or right, is satisfied by the existing "balance."

## The U.S. Opportunity

This is the delicate situation in which the United States must try to exercise discreet influence. Already charged by both the left and the right in the Philippines with having meddled too much in their domestic affairs, Washington will nonetheless have to continue to communicate its concerns to Manila. As the source of support that might make the difference between the Aquino administration's political survival and defeat, the United States has sufficient leverage at least to be given a hearing. The informal exchange of ideas, without publicity, would probably be the best way of communicating American concerns. So far, the Aquino administration appears to be receptive to Washington's counsel.

The United States and the Philippines are security partners in a part of the world that is of strategic importance. As long as that relationship continues, the United States has every reason to contribute to the stability and self-sustained economic growth of the Philippine republic.

It is probably advisable that the United States press for early renegotiation of the Military Bases Agreement. Given the fragility of the coalition in Manila, settling the issue as soon as possible seems prudent. Furthermore, the U.S. Congress has been reluctant to release major funds for repair and enhancement of the facilities until their future is secure. The current arrangement, which terminates in 1991, should be extended a minimum of twenty-five years with provision for periodic review and option for renewal.

U.S. communication agencies should provide information on the functions of the bases to the Philippine public. There is evidence that an informed public in the Philippines would be an ally in the renegotiation.[29]

## Incentives for Renegotiation

The United States should be flexible. It should be ready to provide some compensation, for example, if Manila is willing to begin renegotiation early. One possible form of compensation might be a reconsideration of Washington's position on "parity rights" for American investors in the Philippines. For many years, Filipinos have objected to the U.S. insistence that American investors be granted the same rights as Filipinos in the exploitation of the resources, and in the ownership of public utilities, in the archipelago. Washington insisted on such a provision in commercial or trade agreements even after the islands received their independence. The Philippine Trade Act of 1946 and the Laurel-Langley Agreement of 1954, for example, both contained such a provision.[30] To accommodate Washington's insistence on the issue, the Philippine government was forced to amend its own constitution.

Many Filipinos continue to hold that the parity arrangements violate Philippine sovereignty. Even the Marcos administration was unable to negotiate a new trade treaty with the United States, however beneficial it might have been, because of Washington's intransigence on the parity provision. It might now be time for the United States to concede something in this matter.

Other gestures could be made. The invitation to Corazon Aquino to visit Washington in the fall of 1986 was one such gesture. However lacking in substance the visit might have been, it contributed to the political credibility of the Aquino administration and provided some insulation against domestic critics who object to any readiness to enter into constructive negotiations with the United States. The United States should do everything it can to deflect criticism from the Aquino government.

Beyond that, the United States should be prepared to provide more substantial compensation than it has in the past for the continued use of the military bases. Washington has often been more generous to other countries where basing rights have been less important.

These measures, together with humanitarian and economic aid, the effort to provide Philippine exports access to the U.S. market, and U.S. intercession with international financial institutions to provide assistance, should be understood as contributions to the security relations between the two countries. The Aquino government must be made to understand the seriousness of purpose that animates U.S. efforts. Vital issues are at stake—issues in which the interests of the two nations are fundamentally compatible. The collapse of the present coalition in Manila into an anti-American, leftist regime would mean wretchedness for the long-suffering Philippine people and a major setback to the security policies of the United States.

As we have seen, the presence of representatives of the Philippine military in the ruling coalition constitutes the best insurance against a feckless or calculated move to the left. The United States should support the Philippine military in every manner compatible with the sovereign dignity and integrity of the Philippine republic. Enhanced military aid, increased access to U.S. training facilities and advisors, more generous opportunities to study and undergo advanced training in the United States—all would contribute to the institutional strength and status of the Armed Forces of the Philippines. Such efforts would constitute an intelligent investment in the future of both the United States and the Republic of the Philippines.

## THE LONGER VIEW

The Philippine archipelago is at a major strategic intersection in the West Pacific. Time has vindicated the judgments of the first Americans who insisted that the islands were of strategic significance. The credible deterrence upon which the peace of the region clearly seems to rest involves those islands and the military facilities they make available.

During the past quarter of a century, the Soviet Union has extended its military reach through and around the Mediterranean, across to the Caribbean, down the west and up the east coast of Africa, and into the Indian Ocean and the South China Sea. In 1985, Moscow negotiated its first fishing agreement with a nation in what used to be considered an American preserve: the South Pacific. The agreement with Kiribati, a new state previously known as the Gilbert Islands, signals a Soviet interest in the broad waters of the South Pacific. The Soviets also requested onshore berthing and servicing privileges from Kiribati, but these were denied. Although the Kiribati agreement was not renewed, it is clear that Soviet efforts will continue in the region.

In 1986, Moscow announced diplomatic relations with the South Pacific archipelagic nation of Vanuatu. Vanuatu, a chain of about eighty islands (the former New Hebrides), attained independence in 1980. It is the first new state of the South Pacific to enter into formal diplomatic relations with the USSR.

At about the same time, Fiji announced that it had agreed to discuss prospects for trade and technical cooperation with the Soviet Union. A fishing agreement is probably forthcoming. It is not clear whether the Soviet Union will receive any onshore privileges if such an agreement is concluded.[31]

The pattern has become evident. Soviet naval vessels will soon begin to make regular appearances in the region. The United States has interpreted Soviet intentions in the South Pacific as "disruptive," but the leaders of the island nations of Vanuatu and Papua New Guinea see the Soviet presence as contributing to a "balance," within which the entire region can remain "non-aligned and independent." Most of the island nations of the South Pacific suffer serious financial and economic problems because of their small size and lack of resources— circumstances that make them vulnerable to Soviet blandishments of aid and economic cooperation. How much that influences their judgments about the advantages of being "non-aligned and independent" is difficult to say.

Recent Soviet initiatives in the Pacific region clearly indicate a long-range policy calculated to make the USSR a major Asian power. To date, its moves into the South Pacific have been cautious—and the U.S. military presence in the Philippines gives the anti-Soviet coalition a significant military advantage. Moreover, most of the new nations in the South Pacific remain indifferent to Soviet overtures. Thus far, the Solomon Islands, Tuvalu, and Western Samoa have spurned Soviet offers of financial aid, but it is unclear what might happen should U.S. forces be withdrawn from the South China Sea and should Washington fail to put together a program of aid and technical assistance for the nations involved.

One thing does appear certain: anything that changes the strategic balance in any region of the globe might have grave consequences. With the loss of the facilities in the Philippines, the security situation would change dramatically, and Soviet initiatives in the South Pacific would have much more ominous implications. Any effort to restore the balance in the area, once lost, would involve burdensome expense.

Maintaining a strategic balance appears to be the necessary condition for avoiding major conflict. In that sense, the changes taking place in East Asia have been threatening. The Soviet military buildup in Asia has altered the international configuration of forces. The policies pursued by four administrations in Washington since the mid-1970s could be understood as efforts to restore some balance.

For at least that reason, the United States was solicitous of the Marcos administration even though many of its policies were ill conceived, politically objectionable, and ineffectually executed. Similarly, it is largely for that reason that the United States has accommodated the leadership in Beijing. The People's Republic of China and the United States seem to share very little other than their mutual concern with the Soviet military threat, however, and it is increasingly apparent that the United States can expect little more in security benefits from the PRC than it had received by the mid-1970s. Since that time, the strategic balance in the West Pacific has depended mainly on the availability of the Philippine bases and on the security partnership involving the United States, Japan, and the Republic of Korea. The search for an alternative to the Philippine military bases indicates that the Republic of China on Taiwan and some of the other smaller nations of the Pacific may prove more important for the deterrent strategy of the United States than the China of Deng Xiaoping. The Republic of Korea, the Republic of China on Taiwan, and the ASEAN states, in particular the Republic of the Philippines, should remain central to the policy concerns of the United States and the other industrialized democracies.[32]

The Philippine bases are critical components in the mosaic of forward strategic defense that has deterred nuclear conflict for more than a generation. They serve our interests and those of the nations of the West Pacific—and our presence there constitutes evidence of our resolve to deter Soviet expansion and military misadventure. Until humankind divines a better means of preserving peace, deterrent defense remains our best hope.

# *Notes*

## CHAPTER ONE

1. For a substantial current account of the Philippines, see David Joel Steinberg, *The Philippines: A Singular and Plural Place* (Boulder, Colo.: Westview, 1982).

2. For a version of the life and work of Mahan, see William E. Livezey, *Mahan on Sea Power* (Norman, Okla.: University of Oklahoma, 1981).

3. Alfred Thayer Mahan, *Retrospect and Prospect: Studies in International Relations Naval and Political* (Boston: Little, Brown, 1902), p. 42; Livezey, *Mahan on Sea Power,* chap. 3.

4. Adrian E. Cristobal and A. James Gregor, "The Philippines and the United States: A Brief History of the Security Connection," *Comparative Strategy, 6,* 1 (1986).

5. See James C. Thomson, Jr., Peter W. Stanley, and John Curtis Perry, *Sentimental Imperialists: The American Experience in East Asia* (New York: Harper and Row, 1981), chap. 8, and Mahan, *Retrospect and Prospect,* p. 34.

6. Livezey, *Mahan on Sea Power,* pp. 185–86.

7. In an article by Mahan, "A Twentieth Century Outlook," that appeared in *Harper's Monthly* in September 1897, he alluded to the coming conflict between the "teeming multitudes of central and northern Asia" and the "representatives of civilization."

8. Mahan, "The Philippines and the Future," *The Independent,* 52 (22 March 1900), p. 698.

9. For a brief biography of Lea, see John Clark Kimball, "Homer Lea—Interloper on History," *U.S. Naval Institute Proceedings, 98,* 4 (April 1972), pp. 194–95.

10. Homer Lea, *The Valor of Ignorance* (New York: Harper and Brothers, 1909), pp. 194–95.

11. Douglas MacArthur, *Reminiscences* (New York: McGraw-Hill, 1964), p. 112.

12. As quoted, U.S. Department of State, *The Philippines,* Publication 5508, Far Eastern Series 66, 1954, p. 5.

13. See the discussion in Mamerto S. Ventura, *United States—Philippine Cooperation and Cross-Purposes: Philippine Post-War Recovery and Reform* (Quezon City: Filipiniana, 1974), pp. 7–9, 12–16, 20, 42.

14. See the discussion in David Bernstein, *The Philippine Story* (New York: Farrar, Strauss, 1947), and the comments by Steinberg, *The Philippines,* p. 59.

15. See Emilio Aguinaldo and Vicente Pacis, *A Second Look at America* (New York: Robert Spelier and Sons, 1957), pp. 227–29.

16. *Military Bases,* 61 Stat. 4019, Treaties and Other International Acts Series 1775, Article 1, Section 3.

17. Ibid., Article 3.

18. See the discussion in Stephen Rosskamm Shalom, *The United States and the Philippines: A Study of Neocolonialism* (Philadelphia: Institute for the Study of Human Issues, 1981), pp. 59–61.

19. As quoted, Roland G. Simbulan, *The Bases of Our Insecurity: A Study of the U.S. Military Bases in the Philippines* (Manila: Balai Fellowship, 1983), p. 74.

20. See the discussion in Emerenciana Y. Arcellana, *The Social and Political Thought of Claro Mayo Recto* (Manila: National Research Council of the Philippines, 1981), chap. 4.

21. See the arguments in *The Benitez Papers on Neutrality,* ed. Conchita Liboro de Benitez (Manila: de Benitez, 1972).

22. See John M. Collins, *American and Soviet Military Trends Since the Cuban Missile Crisis* (Washington: Georgetown University, 1978).

23. See David Holloway, *The Soviet Union and the Arms Race* (New Haven: Yale University, 1983).

24. John M. Collins, *U.S.-Soviet Military Balance 1980–1985* (New York: Pergamon-Brassey's, 1985), p. 3.

25. Lawrence K. Korb, *The FY 1981–1985 Defense Program: Issues and Trends* (Washington: American Enterprise Institute, 1980), and William W. Kaufmann, *The 1986 Defense Budget* (Washington: Brookings Institution, 1985).

26. Michael McGuire, "Soviet Naval Programmes," in Paul Murphy, ed., *Naval Power in Soviet Policy* (Washington: United States Air Force, 1978), p. 90.

27. See Gerard K. Burke, "Backfire: Strategic Implications," *Military Review, 57,* 7 (July 1976), pp. 85–90; William D. O'Neil, "Backfire: Long Shadow on the Sea-Lanes," *United States Naval Institute Proceedings,* March 1977, pp. 26–35.

28. Abram N. Shulsky, "Coercive Diplomacy," in Bradford Dismukes and James McConnel, eds., *Soviet Naval Diplomacy* (New York: Pergamon, 1979), pp. 151–53.

29. Bryan Ranft and Geoffrey Till, *The Sea in Soviet Strategy* (Baltimore: Naval Institute Press, 1983), p. 148.

30. For a discussion of this period, see Frank H. Golay, *The Philippines: Public Policy and National Economic Development* (Ithaca: Cornell University, 1961).

31. See A. James Gregor, *Crisis in the Philippines: A Threat to U.S. Interests* (Washington: Ethics and Public Policy Center, 1984), chaps. 2 and 3.

32. See Lichauco's statement at the time of the constitutional convention that preceded the declaration of martial law. Alejandro Lichauco, *The Lichauco Paper: Imperialism in the Philippines* (New York: Monthly Review, 1973).

33. See the related statements to be found in Jose Veloso Abueva, *Filipino Politics, Nationalism and Emerging Ideologies: Background for Constitution-Making* (Manila: Modern Book, 1972), pp. 143, 162–63, 169–70.

34. Lorenzo M. Tañada, Foreword, in Simbulan, *The Bases of Our Insecurity,* pp. 9–12.

35. Jose Diokno, Preface, in Simbulan, *The Bases of Our Insecurity,* pp. 13–16.

36. William Branigin, "As Talks Approach, Philippine Opposition to the U.S. Bases Grows," *International Herald Tribune,* 5 May 1983.

37. "A Declaration of Unity," *Veritas* (Manila), 6 January 1985.

CHAPTER TWO

1. For the Soviet Pacific Fleet order of battle, see Donald C. Daniel and Gael D. Tarleton, "The Soviet Navy in 1984," *U.S. Naval Institute Proceedings,* May 1985, pp. 90–92, 361–64; *Unclassified Communist Naval Orders of Battle* (Washington: Defense Intelligence Agency, May 1984), pp. viii, 2–6.

2. See the testimony of Rear Admiral John L. Butts, director of naval intelligence, before the Seapower and Force Projection Subcommittee of the Senate Armed Services Committee, 26 February 1985, mimeographed.

3. Bill Hewitt and Melinda Liu, "America's Wobbly Kingpin," *Newsweek,* 20 May 1985, pp. 14–16.

4. See "Carter's Front-Line Fighters," *Far Eastern Economic Review,* 2 June 1978, pp. 24–30; "U.S. Official Cites Bases' 'Crucial Role,' " *Bulletin Today* (Manila), 18 July 1983, p. 1.

5. Alvin J. Cottrell, "Key U.S. Bases in the Philippines," *National Defense,* 67 (December 1982), pp. 31, 34–36.

6. Lawrence E. Grinter, *The Philippine Bases: Continuing Utility in a Changing Strategic Context* (Washington: National Defense University, February 1980).

7. Hungdah Chiu, "South China Sea Islands: Implications for Delimiting the Seabed and Future Shipping Routes," *China Quarterly,* 72 (December 1978), pp. 742–65.

8. As cited, Sheilah Ocampo-Kalfors, "Easing Toward Conflict," *Far Eastern Economic Review,* 28 April 1983, p. 38.

9. Derek W. Bowett, *The Legal Regime of Islands in International Law* (Dobbs Ferry, N.Y.: Ocean Publications, 1979), and Barry Buzan, *A Sea of Troubles? Sources of Dispute in the New Ocean Regime,* Adelphi Papers, no. 143 (London: International Institute for Strategic Studies, 1978).

10. See the discussion in F. A. Vallat, "Continental Shelf," *British Yearbook of International Law, 23* (1946), pp. 333–34.

11. See Ying-jeou Ma, *Legal Problems of Seabed Boundary Delimitation in the East China Sea,* Occasional Papers/Reprints in Contemporary Asian Studies, no. 3 (Baltimore: University of Maryland School of Law, 1984).

12. Hungdah Chiu, *Chinese Attitude Toward Continental Shelf and Its Implication on Delimiting Seabed in Southeast Asia* (Baltimore: University of Maryland School of Law, 1977), pp. 28–29.

13. See Phiphat Tangsubkul, *ASEAN and the Law of the Sea* (Singapore: Institute of Southeast Asian Studies, 1982), chap. 1.

14. "Chinese Representative Speaks at ECAFE Meeting," *Beijing Review, 17,* 6–7 (12 April 1974).

15. Tangsubkul, *ASEAN and the Law of the Sea,* p. 15.

16. Ma, *Legal Problems,* p. 89.

17. Hungdah Chiu, *China and the Law of the Sea Conference,* Occasional Papers/Reprints in Contemporary Asian Studies, no. 3 (Baltimore: University of Maryland School of Law, 1981), p. 17.

18. See, for example, Hiroshi Niino and K. O. Emery, "Sediments of Shallow Portions of East China and South China Sea," *American Geological Society Bulletin* (1961), pp. 731–43.

19. See the summary discussion in Orville Shell, *To Get Rich Is Glorious: China in the 80s* (New York: Mentor, 1986), pp. 210–11.

20. See Martin H. Katchen, "The Spratly Islands and the Law of the Sea: 'Dangerous Ground' for Asian Peace," *Asian Survey, 17,* 12 (December 1977), pp. 1167–81.

21. Harold C. Hinton, *The China Sea: The American Stake in Its Future* (New York: National Strategy Information Center, 1980), p. 23.

22. Nayan Chanda, "The Deep Freeze," *Far Eastern Economic Review,* 14 June 1984, p. 17.

23. See "Where the Guns May Be Turned on Oil Driller," *Business Week,* 9 May 1983, p. 44.

24. Foreign Broadcast Information Service, Asia and Pacific, 2 May 1984, p. K14.

25. See the discussion in G. Jacobs, "New Soviet Arms for Vietnam," *Pacific Defense Reporter,* September 1982, p. 51.

26. Richard D. Fisher, *Brewing Conflict in the South China Sea,* Asian Studies Center Backgrounder (Washington: Heritage Foundation, 25 October 1984).

27. K. Das, "Perched on a Claim," *Far Eastern Economic Review,* 29 September 1983, p. 40.

28. Selig S. Harrison, *China, Oil, and Asia: Conflicts Ahead?* (New York: Columbia University, 1977), p. 139.

29. See Jusuf Wanandi, "Security in the Asia-Pacific Region: An Indonesian Observation," *Asian Survey,* December 1978, p. 1214, and "Conflict and Cooperation in the Asia-Pacific Region: An Indonesian Perspective," *Asian Survey,* June 1982, p. 513; Lee Boon Hick, "Constraints on Singapore's Foreign Policy," ibid., p. 528; Tom Breen, "Area Needs U.S. Bases, Australian Tells Aquino," *Washington Times,* 27 May 1986, p. 5A.

## CHAPTER THREE

1. Alvin J. Cottrell and Robert J. Hanks, *The Military Utility of the U.S. Facilities in the Philippines* (Washington: Georgetown University, 1980), pp. 6–7.

2. See William Emerson Berry, Jr., *American Military Bases in the Philippines, Base Negotiations, and Philippine-American Relations: Past, Present and Future* (Washington: U.S. Government Printing Office, May 1981), pp. 445–50.

3. A. James Gregor, "The Key Role of U.S. Bases in the Philippines," Asian Studies Center Backgrounder (Washington: Heritage Foundation, 10 January 1984), p. 5.

4. Berry, *American Military Bases,* pp. 449–50.

5. Joseph Lelyveld, "U.S. Military Presence in Asia as of Old, but Justification for It Is All New," *New York Times,* 26 January 1974, p. 1.

6. "Finger-Tip Facts About Subic Bay," Backgrounder (Subic Bay: U.S. Naval Base Press Information, April 1978), p. C-3.

7. U.S. Congress, Senate, Committee on Foreign Relations, Subcommittee on Foreign Assistance, *United States–Philippines Base Negotiations,* Staff Report, 7 April 1977, pp. 11–12.

8. *Clark Air Base Guide* (Manila: USAF 3rd Tactical Fighter Wing Public Affairs Office, 1984), p. 5.

9. Michael Bedford, "The Philippines: The Bases of U.S. Intervention," *Defense and Disarmament News,* October-November 1985, p. 4.

10. See the *Exchange of Notes Amending the Philippine-U.S. Military Bases Agreement of 1947,* 7 January 1979, and *Memorandum of Agreement,* 1 June 1983.

11. "U.S.-Philippine Relations: Basis for the Bases," *Far Eastern Economic Review,* 13 May 1977, p. 30.

12. Serapio P. Taccad, "Philippine-American Relations and the U.S. Bases: A Filipino Perspective," *Naval War College Review,* 30 (Spring 1978), p. 73.

13. See Conchita Liboro de Benitez, ed., *The Benitez Papers on Neutrality* (Manila: de Benitez, 1972).

14. See Mamerto S. Ventura, *United States–Philippine Cooperation and Cross-Purposes: Philippine Post-War Recovery and Reform* (Quezon City: Filipiniana, 1974), pp. 100–103.

15. See the entire discussion in Roland G. Simbulan, *The Bases of Our Insecurity: A Study of the U.S. Military Bases in the Philippines* (Manila: Balai Fellowship, 1983), chap. 5.

16. Ibid., p. 11.

17. Ibid., pp. 14–15.

18. These sentiments appear so regularly among responsible Filipinos that the U.S. Embassy in Manila found it prudent to respond publicly to them. See Herbert S. Malin, "Myths and Realities About U.S. Bases in R.P.," *Philippine Daily Express* (Manila), 27 March 1983, p. 5.

CHAPTER FOUR

1. See A. James Gregor, *Crisis in the Philippines: A Threat to U.S. Interests* (Washington: Ethics and Public Policy Center, 1984), pp. 42–43.

2. Leonor M. Briones, *The Philippine Debt Burden: Who Borrows? Who Pays?* (Manila: Aklat Pilipino, 1984), p. 3.

3. *What Crisis? Highlights of the Philippine Economy 1983* (Manila: Ibon Databank, 1984), pp. 4–5, 24.

4. See Emmanual S. De Dios, ed., *An Analysis of the Philippine Economic Crisis* (Quezon City: University of the Philippines, 1984), pp. 3, 9, 51.

5. See *Foreign Economic Trends and Their Implications for the United States: Philippines* (Washington: International Trade Administration, December 1982).

6. *Makati Business Club Economic Balance Sheet,* March 1983, p. 5.

7. See J. P. Estanislao, *Our Flaws Are Showing* (Manila: Center for Research and Communication, December 1983).

8. *Social Weather Station Survey of Metro Manila, July 1982: Final Report* (Manila: Development Academy of the Philippines, 21 October 1982).

9. *Public Opinion Poll of Luzon 1983* (Manila: Development Academy of the Philippines, 5 October 1983; confidential); *Public Opinion Poll of Visayas and Mindanao 1983* (Manila: Development Academy of the Philippines, 25 August 1983).

10. The difference was not statistically significant. *The BBC Nationwide Sociopolitical Opinion Surveys of 1984 and 1985* (Manila: The Bishops-Businessmen's Conference for Human Development, August 1985), pp. 2, 16.

11. *Report on the PSSC National Opinion Survey of September 1985* (Quezon City: Philippine Social Science Council, 14 December 1985), pp. 17–18. Compare the results with *Project "Polls-NCR"* (Quezon City: President's Center for Special Studies, 15 May 1985).

12. See U.S. Congress, Senate, Select Committee on Intelligence, *The Philippines: A Situation Report*, Dave Holliday et al., Staff Report, 31 October 1985.

13. See De Dios, *Analysis of the Economic Crisis*, Appendix One, pp. 83–87.

14. Veronica Huang Li, "The Philippines Under Stress," *Editorial Research Report, 1980* (Washington: Washington Congressional Quarterly, 1980), 2, 15, p. 767.

15. Carl H. Lande, "Philippine Prospects After Martial Law," *Foreign Affairs*, 59 (Summer 1981), 1164.

16. *White Paper on the Communist Insurgency in the Philippines* (Manila: Ministry of National Defense, 11 May 1985).

17. U.S. Congress, Senate, Committee on Foreign Relations, *Insurgency and Counterinsurgency in the Philippines*, November 1985, p. 2.

18. See Romulo F. Yap, *Insurgency* (Manila: Command and General Staff College, February 1985), pp. 34–35.

19. Larry A. Niksch, *Insurgency and Counterinsurgency in the Philippines* (Washington: Congressional Research Service, 1 July 1985), p. 7.

20. Renato Constantino, *The Nationalist Alternative* (Quezon City: Foundation for Nationalist Studies, 1979), pp. 3, 4, 71, 81, passim.

21. Rosalinda Pineda-Ofreneo, ed., *Foreign Capital and the Philippine Crisis: An Unassembled Symposium* (Quezon City: International Studies Institute of the Philippines, 1985), which contains the responses of these scholars to questions about the relationship between the "imperialist" U.S. and the Philippines. Quoted material appears on pp. 1, 9, 37, 70–71, 79.

22. See, for example, Diokno's introduction to Edberto M. Villegas, *Studies in Philippine Political Economy* (Manila: Silangan, 1983), and his introduction to *What Crisis?*

23. Letizia R. Constantino, ed., *Issues Without Tears: A Layman's Manual of Current Issues* (Quezon City: Education Forum, 1984), 3, pp. 69–70. See the remaining volumes for the educational discussion of "capitalist" exploitation of the Philippines.

24. Leif Rosenberger, "Philippine Communism and the Soviet Union," *Survey*, 29, 1 (Spring 1985), p. 142; see also p. 131.

25. See Guy Sacerdoti and Philip Bowring, "Marx, Mao, and Marcos," *Far Eastern Economic Review*, 21 November 1985, pp. 52–59.

26. *The State of the Nation After Three Years of Martial Law, September 21, 1975* (San Francisco: Civil Liberties Union of the Philippines, 1976), pp. 24–25.

27. Fred Poole and Max Vanzi, *Revolution in the Philippines: The United States in a Hall of Cracked Mirrors* (New York: McGraw-Hill, 1984), chap. 11.

28. Ibid., pp. 120–21, 142, 204, 311.

29. See Robert Pringle, *Indonesia and the Philippines: American Interests in Island Southeast Asia* (New York: Columbia University, 1980), p. 57.

30. *BBC Nationwide Sociopolitical Opinion Surveys,* p. 21.

⌣31. See "Marcos Foes Announce Unity Platform," *New York Times,* 27 December 1984, p. A3.

32. Letizia Constantino, *Issues Without Tears,* 3, pp. 69–70.

33. See the discussion in Tom Marks, "Don't Discount the Philippine Communists," *Asian Wall Street Journal,* 28 April 1986, p. 6.

34. Bernardo M. Villegas et al., *The Philippines at a Crossroad: Some Vision for the Nation* (Manila: Center for Research and Communication, 1985).

35. Marks, "Don't Discount the Philippine Communists."

36. U.S. Congress, Senate, Select Committee on Intelligence, *The Philippines,* p. 16.

37. *Project "Polls-NCR,"* p. x; *BBC Nationwide Sociopolitical Opinion Surveys,* p. 16; *Report on the PSSC National Opinion Survey,* p. 32.

38. See "Big Bases, Big Bucks in the Philippines," *Life, 9,* 6 (June 1986), pp. 47–52.

39. Ross H. Munro, "Dateline Manila: Moscow's Next Win?," *Foreign Policy,* 56 (Fall 1984), pp. 173–90.

## CHAPTER FIVE

1. A recent reiteration of these mission assignments is found in Secretary of Defense Caspar Weinberger's *Annual Report to the Congress, Fiscal Year 1986.*

2. See Alva M. Bowen, *The Philippine Bases: U.S. Redeployment Options* (Washington: Congressional Research Service, 20 February 1986).

3. The studies undertaken to explore the options available include: Cheri Lynn Connilogue, *New Bases for Old: An Unusual View of the Philippine Bases Problem* (Monterey: Naval Postgraduate School, December 1984, M.A. thesis); Alvin Cottrell and Thomas H. Moorer, *U.S. Overseas Bases: Problems of Projecting Military Power Abroad* (Beverly Hills: Sage, 1977); Lawrence E. Grinter, *The Philippine Bases: Continuing Utility in a Changing Strategic Context* (Washington: National Defense University, February 1980); Clifford Krieger and Robert E. Webb, *The Strategic Importance of U.S. Military Facilities in the Republic of the Philippines* (Carlisle Barracks, Pa.: U.S. Army War College, May 1983); and Edmund Gannon, *Alternative Sites for U.S. Philippine Bases* (Washington: Congressional Research Service, 1977).

4. Alvin J. Cottrell and Robert J. Hanks, *The Military Utility of the U.S. Facilities in the Philippines* (Washington: Georgetown University, 1980), pp. 13–14.

124    NOTES TO PAGES 73–87

5. See the discussion in Jack Anderson, "Alternatives to Philippine Bases Sought," *Washington Post,* 3 December 1985, p. B13.

6. See U.S. Congress, Joint Senate-House Armed Services Subcommittee, *Hearings on CVN-70 Aircraft Carrier,* Desmond P. Wilson, Jr., 1970, p. 574.

7. *Alternatives to the Northern Marianas Islands Land Lease* (Washington: General Accounting Office, 9 August 1983).

8. Stanley S. Bedlington, *Malaysia and Singapore: The Building of New States* (Ithaca, N.Y.: Cornell University, 1978), pp. 248–49.

9. Cottrell and Hanks, *Military Utility,* p. 12.

10. See Sheldon W. Simon, *The ASEAN States and Regional Security* (Stanford: Hoover Institution, 1982), pp. 116–17.

11. See the discussion in Robert C. Horn, *The Soviet Threat in Southeast Asia: Illusion or Reality?* (Kuala Lumpur: Institute of Strategic and International Studies, 1985).

12. Mohamed Noordin Sopiee, *The Russian Threat: Between Alarm and Complacency* (Kuala Lumpur: Institute of Strategic and International Studies, 1985), p. 15.

13. Bowen, *The Philippine Bases,* p. 31.

14. L. Bruce Swanson, Jr., "The Navy of the People's Republic of China," in Barry M. Blechman and Robert P. Berman, eds., *Guide to Far Eastern Navies* (Annapolis: Naval Institute, 1978), pp. 122–23.

15. See the discussion in David G. Muller, Jr., *China as a Maritime Power* (Boulder, Colo.: Westview, 1983), pp. 182–84.

16. Foreign Broadcast Information Service, China, 19 June 1985, p. G3.

17. Martin Lasater, "Is Beijing Playing Its Moscow Card?," Asian Studies Center Backgrounder (Washington: Heritage Foundation, 23 October 1985).

18. See *Far Eastern Economic Review,* 28 March 1985, p. 10.

19. *Asian Security 1985* (Tokyo: Research Institute for Peace and Security, 1985), pp. 41–42.

20. See A. James Gregor, *The China Connection: U.S. Policy and the People's Republic of China* (Stanford: Hoover Institution, 1986), chaps. 4 and 5.

21. Donald Hugh McMillen, "Chinese Perspectives on International Security," in Donald Hugh McMillen, ed., *Asian Perspectives on International Security* (New York: St. Martin's, 1984), pp. 173–94.

22. Muller, *China as a Maritime Power,* pp. 231–35.

23. See A. James Gregor and Maria Hsia Chang, *The Republic of China and U.S. Policy: A Study in Human Rights* (Washington: Ethics and Public Policy Center, 1983).

24. Taiwan Relations Act, Public Law 96-8, 10 April 1979, section 2(b), paragraphs 2 and 4.

25. See the discussion in Edwin K. Snyder, A. James Gregor, and Maria Hsia Chang, *The Taiwan Relations Act and the Defense of the Republic of China* (Berkeley: Institute of International Studies, 1980).

26. William J. Durch, "The Navy of the Republic of China," in Blechman and Berman, *Guide to Far Eastern Navies,* pp. 246–47.

27. Norman Chao-hsin Wei, "The Prospective Development of Shipping Industry and Marine Transportation in Taiwan, Republic of China" (Communi-

cation at the Asia-Pacific Sea Lanes of Communication Security Conference, Singapore, 2–5 May 1985).

28. This argument goes back as far as Michael Pillsbury's piece, "U.S.-Chinese Military Ties," *Foreign Policy,* no. 20 (Fall 1975), p. 51.

29. See U.S. Congress, House, Committee on Foreign Affairs, *Hearings, United States–China Relations,* testimony of James A. Kelly, deputy assistant secretary of defense for East Asia and Pacific affairs, 5 June 1984, p. 193.

30. See the testimony of Banning Garrett in *The United States and the People's Republic of China: Issues for the 1980s* (Washington: Government Printing Office, 1980), p. 98.

31. William T. Tow, "The U.S., PRC, and Japan: Military Technology Transfer Policies and Strategic Collaboration" (Communication at the Fifteenth Sino-American Conference on Mainland China, Taipei, 8–14 June 1986), pp. 8–9.

32. Caspar Weinberger, *Annual Report to the Congress, Fiscal Year 1983* (Washington: U.S. Government Printing Office, 1982), pp. 11–21.

33. See Kenneth Lieberthal, "Domestic Politics and Foreign Policy," in Harry Harding, ed., *China's Foreign Relations in the 1980s* (New Haven: Yale University, 1984), pp. 64–65.

34. See A. James Gregor, *Three Essays on China Policy and U.S. Security Interests in East Asia* (Berkeley: Pacific Basin Project, July 1985).

35. See Paul H. B. Godwin, "Soldiers and Statesmen in Conflict: Chinese Defense and Foreign Policies in the 1980s," in Samuel S. Kim, ed., *China and the World: Chinese Foreign Policy in the Post-Mao Era* (Boulder, Colo.: Westview, 1984), pp. 215–34.

## CHAPTER SIX

1. For some of the background of the U.S.-Philippine relationship, see the essays in A. James Gregor, ed., *The U.S. and the Philippines: A Challenge to a Special Relationship* (Washington: Heritage Foundation, 1983).

2. The Aquino government presented an outline of its economic program to the Asian Development Bank as part of its effort to reschedule outstanding loans. See Foreign Broadcast Information Service, Asia and Pacific, 6 May 1986, p. P3; also 25 March 1986, p. P20, and 14 April 1986, pp. P8–10.

3. See the testimony of Gustav Ranis, *The Situation and Outlook in the Philippines* (Washington: Government Printing Office, 20 September 1984), pp. 41–46.

4. See the detailed articles in the *Philippines Yearbook* for 1982–83 and that for 1983–84 (Manila: Fookien Times, 1982 and 1983).

5. See Gerald M. Boyd, "Discord Reported as Reagan Meets Aquino's Deputy," *New York Times,* 2 May 1986, p. 8.

6. Secretary of State George Shultz as reported in Marvin Howe, "Shultz Endorses Aquino Government," *New York Times,* 5 June 1986, p. 3.

7. Foreign Broadcast Information Service, Asia and Pacific, 17 April 1986, p. P8.

8. See Allen Weinstein, "Yes, the U.S. Can Afford to Help Manila," *New York Times,* 18 May 1986, p. 25.

9. Seth Mydans, "Philippine Military Chief Asserts the Rebels Have Resumed Fight," *New York Times,* 5 June 1986, p. 1.

10. Foreign Broadcast Information Service, Asia and Pacific, 18 March 1986, p. P21.

11. Jose P. Magno and A. James Gregor, "Insurgency and Counterinsurgency in the Philippines," *Asian Survey, 26,* 5 (May 1986), pp. 501–17.

12. See the discussion in Larry A. Niksch, "The U.S. in Contemporary Southeast Asia" (Communication at the Conference on Changing International Relations in Asia, Institute of Asian Studies, St. John's University, 26–27 October 1984).

13. See Napoleon Valeriano and Charles T. R. Bohannan, *Counter-Guerrilla Operations: The Philippines Experience* (New York: Praeger, 1961).

14. See Stephen R. Shalom, "Counterinsurgency in the Philippines," *Journal of Contemporary Asia, 7,* 2 (1977), pp. 157–64.

15. See Larry Niksch, "Special Report on the Philippines," *Wharton Pacific Basin Economic Service, 2,* 5 (15 March 1985); U.S. Congress, Senate, Select Committee on Intelligence, *The Philippines: A Situation Report,* Dave Holliday et al., Staff Report, 31 October 1985; "Reagan Security Advisor Sees Communist Takeover in Philippines," *Asia Cable, 2,* 11 (13 September 1985), pp. 1–3.

16. For the text of the document, see U.S. Congress, House, Subcommittee on Asian and Pacific Affairs, *United States–Philippines Relations and the New Base and Air Agreement,* 17, 23, 28 June 1983, pp. 117–18.

17. Foreign Broadcast Information Service, Asia and Pacific, 5 March 1986, p. P18.

18. See Seth Mydans, "Grumbling in the Philippines: Can Aquino Govern Nation?," *New York Times,* 21 April 1986, pp. 1 and 6.

19. Foreign Broadcast Information Service, Asia and Pacific, 3 December 1985, p. P6.

20. "UNIDO Suggests 'Alternative,' " *Bulletin Today* (Manila), 27 May 1983, p. 1.

21. For the complete text of "A Declaration of Unity," see *Veritas* (Manila), 6 January 1985.

22. "Fifteen Point Plan," *Malaya* (Manila), 21 January 1981, p. 1.

23. "8,000 Hit U.S. Bases in Angeles Rally," *Bulletin Today* (Manila), 14 June 1983, p. 36.

24. "Marcos Foes Announce United Platform," *New York Times,* 27 December 1984, p. A3.

25. See William Branigan, "As Talks Approach, Philippine Opposition to U.S. Bases Grows," *International Herald Tribune,* 5 May 1983; "Group Hits U.S. Bases," *Bulletin Today* (Manila), 11 May 1983, p. 32; C. Almoria, Jr., "Nuclear Danger to RP Cited," ibid., 8 May 1983, p. 1.

26. Foreign Broadcast Information Service, Asia and Pacific, 24 March 1986, pp. P1–2. But see her later insistence that the Philippines do not need the U.S. bases: Clayton Jones, "Aquino Interview: We're Safe Without U.S. Bases," *Christian Science Monitor,* 25 July 1986, p. 1.

27. See "Giving Peace Another Chance," *Asia Week,* 12 (4 May 1986), p. 21; Seth Mydans, "Philippine Military Chief Asserts the Rebels Have Resumed Fight," *New York Times,* 5 June 1986, p. 1.

28. Foreign Broadcast Information Service, Asia and Pacific, 18 April 1986, pp. P6–7.

29. In the most extensive survey of Philippine attitudes toward the U.S. bases, the majority of those who claimed to be informed on the issues voted for a continued U.S. presence. *Report on the PSSC National Opinion Survey of September 1985,* pp. 32–33.

30. See the discussion in Frank H. Golay, *The Philippines: Public Policy and National Economic Development* (Ithaca, N.Y.: Cornell University, 1961), pp. 64–66. See also Aurelio B. Calderon, *The Laurel-Langley Agreement: A Critically Annotated and Selected Bibliography* (Manila: De La Salle University, 1979).

31. See Francis Daniel, "Slowly, Soviets Move to Expand Presence in South Pacific," *Washington Times,* 1 July 1986, p. 4D.

32. See the argument in A. James Gregor and Maria Hsia Chang, *The Iron Triangle: A U.S. Security Policy for Northeast Asia* (Stanford: Hoover Institution, 1984).

# Index of Names

129